MAXIMIZE YOUR WRITING

1

Maximize Your Writing 1

Copyright © 2017 by Pearson Education, Inc.

Pearson Education, Inc., 221 River Street, Hoboken, NJ 07030 USA

Staff credits: The people who made up the **Maximize Your Writing** team are Pietro Alongi, Rhea Banker, Tracey Munz Cataldo, Mindy DePalma, Gina DiLillo, Niki Lee, Amy McCormick, Lindsay Richman, and Paula Van Ells.

Text composition: MPS North America LLC
Design: EMC Design Ltd
Photo credit: Cover, PHOTOCREO Michal Bednarek / Shutterstock

ISBN-13: 978-0-13-466143-8   ISBN-10: 0-13-466143-5

Printed in the United States of America
2   16

pearsonelt.com/maximizeyourwriting

CONTENTS

Writing Level 1 – Beginner

Pre-Test 1

In Pre-Test 1, you will demonstrate how well you understand sentence structure, grammar, punctuation, mechanics, and organization. You have 50 minutes to complete the test. Circle the letter of the correct answer.

1 Sima is from Kiev. It is _____ capital of Ukraine.

    a a

    b an

    c the

    d some

2 I can meet you ___ 7:00 P.M.

    a in

    b on

    c at

    d of

3 Sonia lives _____ First Street.

    a in

    b on

    c at

    d next

4 Do you have _____ about the conference?

    a information

    b an information

    c informations

    d the informations

5 The information _____ not correct.

    a was

    b were

    c am

    d are

6 Next weekend we _____ our garage.

    a cleaning

    b are going to clean

    c clean

    d cleaned

7 The movie will start _____ ten minutes.

    a this

    b next

    c in

    d from

8 The food at that restaurant _____ not expensive.

    a is

    b are

    c am

    d be

9 The baby _____ in the afternoon.

    a not sleep

    b doesn't sleep

    c no sleep

    d no sleeping

10 We usually _____ the house at 7:30 A.M., but today we left at 9:00 A.M.

    a leave

    b are leaving

    c will leave

    d left

11 The weather _____ very cold last week.

    a was

    b is

    c be

    d were

12 Carlos _____ the project yesterday.

    a finishing

    b finish

    c finishes

    d finished

13 The guests _____ about an hour ago.

    a leave

    b leaves

    c left

    d leaved

14 There _____ a white cat on the porch.

    a be

    b are

    c is

    d were

15 _____ classes on weekends.

   a There no

   b Are no

   c There are no

   d No are

16 I love my new car. ___ fun to drive.

   a Its

   b It's

   c Its'

   d It

17 I borrowed _____ dictionary.

   a Linda'

   b Linda's

   c Lindas

   d Lindas'

18 Circle the letter of the correct sentence.

   a the mail is late today

   b The mail is late today

   c the mail is late today.

   d The mail is late today.

19 Circle the letter of the answer with correct capital letters.

   a I don't want to visit chicago in the Winter.

   b I don't want to visit Chicago in the Winter.

   c I don't want to visit Chicago in the winter.

   d I don't want to visit chicago in the winter.

20 Circle the letter of the sentence with correct punctuation.

   a I will buy a car, if I get a good job.

   b I will buy a car if I get a good job.

   c I will buy, a car if I get a good job.

   d I will buy a car if, I get a good job.

21 Circle the letter of the sentence with correct punctuation.

   a The shoes are ugly, and they hurt my feet.

   b The shoes are ugly and they hurt my feet.

   c The shoes are ugly and, they hurt my feet.

   d The shoes, are ugly and they hurt my feet.

22 Circle the letter of the sentence with correct punctuation.

   a Last month Janet went on three business trips.

   b Last month Janet went on three business trips.

   c Last month, Janet went on three business trips.

   d Last month Janet, went on three business trips.

23 Yoshi works in the daytime, _____ he goes to school at night.

a if

b only

c or

d and

24 Maxine loves to eat, _____ she hates to cook.

a and

b but

c or

d so

25 My apartment is big, _____ it is very dark.

a or

b if

c so

d but

26 I will walk to work, _____ I will ride my bike.

a or

b and

c so

d but

27 Lin doesn't have a car, _____ he takes the bus to work.

a and

b or

c only

d so

28 Which sentence is correct? Circle the letter of the correct answer.

a Susannah will stay home if she is sick.

b Susannah stay home if she will be sick.

c Susannah will stay home if she will be sick.

d Susannah stay home if she sick.

29 Which sentence is correct? Circle the letter of the correct answer.

a I will be sad, when you go.

b When you go I will be sad.

c You go, when I will be sad.

d I will be sad when you go.

30 Which sentence is correct? Circle the letter of the correct answer.

a I went to bed early. Because I was very tired.

b I went to bed early, because I was very tired.

c I went to bed early because I was very tired.

d I went to bed early because, I was very tired.

31 Which sentence is correct? Circle the letter of the correct answer.

a The sun went down, after, we turned on the lights.

b After the sun went down, we turned on the lights.

c The sun went down, after we turned on the lights.

d After the sun went down we turned on the lights.

32 Which sentence is correct? Circle the letter of the correct answer.

a The children washed their hands, before they ate lunch.

b The children washed their hands. Before they ate lunch.

c The children washed their hands, before, they ate lunch.

d The children washed their hands before they ate lunch.

33 Which sentence is correct? Circle the letter of the correct answer.

a I will wash the car, then I will take a nap.

b I will wash the car then I will take a nap.

c I will wash the car. Then I will take a nap.

d I will wash the car, I will take a nap.

34 Most of the work ____ finished.

a am

b is

c are

d be

35 To make a great cup of coffee, follow these steps. _____ , boil the water.

a Begin

b To begin

c At start

d First all

36 I'm going to do three things today. First, I'm going to go to the gym. After that, I'm going to meet my girlfriend for lunch. _____ , I'm going to study for my English test.

a For example

b And

c Most importantly

d Therefore

37 Read the paragraph. Circle the letter of the sentence that doesn't belong.

1) Giraffes are very unusual animals. 2) First, they are the tallest animals on earth. 3) An adult male giraffe can grow to be eighteen feet tall! 4) Next, giraffes are covered in dark patches. 5) The color of the patches depends on what the giraffe eats and where it lives. 6) There is a giraffe at the zoo in my city. 7) Third, giraffes don't sleep much. 8) They only sleep for five or ten minutes at a time, and they can sleep standing up.

  a Sentence 1
  b Sentence 3
  c Sentence 6
  d Sentence 8

38 There are two reasons why I do not eat beef. _____ I believe beef is not healthy.

  a For example,
  b In the beginning,
  c One reason is that
  d Because

39 The San Diego Zoo has many unusual animals. _____ , you can see a giant panda there.

  a At first
  b For instance
  c One
  d Because

40 Read the topic sentence for a paragraph. Which words tell you what the paragraph will discuss? Circle the letter of the correct answer.

Topic Sentence: People in different cultures have different ways of greeting each other when they meet.

  a people
  b different cultures
  c different ways of greeting each other
  d when they meet

Pre-Test 2

In Pre-Test 2, you will demonstrate how well you can write about a topic. Pay attention to sentence structure, grammar, punctuation, mechanics, organization, and vocabulary. Write about the following topic or the topic your teacher assigns. You have 50 minutes to complete the test.

Write a paragraph about why you are studying English. When and why did you decide to study English? What are you doing now to continue your study of English? How are you going to use English in the future?

PUNCTUATION AND MECHANICS

Apostrophes

CONTRACTIONS WITH AUXILIARY BE AND DO

Presentation

Apostrophes: Contractions with Auxiliary *Be* and *Do*

The auxiliary verbs *be* and *do* can be contracted. Use an apostrophe to create a contraction. The apostrophe replaces a letter in a contraction.

	Rules	Examples
Affirmative contractions with *be*	I + am = I'm	**I'm** ready.
	he + is = he's	**He's** a student.
	she + is = she's	**She's** Japanese.
	it + is = it's	**It's** his car.
	that + is = that's	**That's** his sister.
	we + are = we're	**We're** from Canada.
	you + are = you're	**You're** my teacher.
	they + are = they're	**They're** our cousins.
Negative contractions with *be*	is + not = isn't	He **isn't** married.
	are + not = aren't	They **aren't** going.
Negative contractions with *do*	does + not = doesn't	He **doesn't** understand.
	do + not = don't	We **don't** know the answer.

Practice 1

Rewrite the underlined phrase as a contraction.

Example:

1 *It is* _____It's_____ *Monday.*

2 Sara is my neighbor. <u>She is</u> _____ a teacher.

3 Bob and Carol <u>are not</u> _____ coming to the party.

4 Yuki and I are roommates. <u>We are</u> _____ good friends.

5 The mailman <u>does not</u> _____ come on Sundays.

6 <u>I am</u> _____ not ready for the test.

7 My new car is small, and <u>it is</u> _____ easy to drive.

8 Cats <u>do not</u> _____ like to swim.

9 Don't wait for them. <u>They are</u> _____ not ready.

10 I like driving with you. <u>You are</u> _____ a good driver.

11 Don't use that pot. It <u>is not</u> _____ clean.

Practice 2

Read the following sentences. Circle eight errors with contractions.

1 Mrs. Kurtz: Hello. My name is Mrs. Kurtz. Im the new English teacher.

   Student: Hi. My name is Rana, and this is Katya. I think were in your class.

   Mrs. Kurtz: It's nice to meet you both.

2 Student: Sorry Mrs. Kurtz, but I dont have my grammar book with me.

   Mrs. Kurtz: That's OK. You can share a book with another student.

3 Mrs. Kurtz: Is Sonia Cruz here today?

   Student: No, she isnt.

   Mrs. Kurtz: Where is she? Is she sick?

   Student: No, I think she's with her parents. Theyre visiting from Peru.

4 Student 1: Are we having a test tomorrow?

   Student 2: No, we arent. Mrs. Kurtz cancelled it.

5 Student 1: Is something wrong with your phone?

   Student 2: It doesnt work. The battery is dead.

6 A: I know you. You're in my English class, right?

   B: Yes, I am.

   A: Do you like the class?

   B: I really like the teacher. Hes good.

POSSESSIVES

Presentation

Apostrophes: Possessives

Possessive nouns show that something belongs to somebody. Follow these spelling rules for possessives.

Rules	Examples
Add apostrophe + -s to singular nouns.	Jerry's bike, Martha's brother
Add apostrophe + -s to plural nouns that do not end in -s.	the children's room, people's names
Add apostrophe (without -s) to plural nouns that end in -s.	the students' answers, the Fongs' house

Practice 1

Rewrite the underlined word as a possessive noun.

Example:

1 *A job that belongs to my* <u>mother</u> = *my* _____*mother's*_____ *job*
2 A last name that belongs to <u>Linda</u> = _____ last name
3 The pants that belong to the <u>man</u> = the _____ pants
4 The pants that belong to the <u>men</u> = the _____ pants
5 The houses that belong to my <u>neighbors</u> = my _____ houses
6 The family that belongs to my <u>roommate</u> = my _____ family
7 The beds that belong to my <u>dogs</u> = my _____ beds
8 The toy that belongs to the <u>child</u> = the _____ toy
9 The toys that belong to the <u>children</u> = the _____ toys
10 The desk that belongs to the <u>teacher</u> = the _____ desk
11 The names that belong to the <u>teachers</u> = the _____ names

Practice 2

Read each sentence. Decide if the sentence needs a possessive noun or a plural noun. Underline the correct form.

Example:

1 *The girls/<u>girls'</u> rooms are very neat.*
2 The professors/professors' offices are on the second floor.
3 We're having dinner at the Smiths/Smiths' house.
4 My grandparents/grandparents' live in Michigan.
5 It was the students/students' idea.
6 Richard and Steven are boys/boys' names.
7 All the wives/wives' have blond hair.
8 All my brothers/brothers' wives have blond hair.
9 The dogs/dogs' names are Rex and Spank.
10 There are six desks/desks' in each row.
11 The test questions/questions' were too difficult for me.

Capital Letters
BEGINNING A SENTENCE

Presentation

Capital Letters at the Beginning of Sentences

Every sentence in English begins with a capital letter. Do not use capital letters in the middle of a sentence, except with the pronoun *I* and with proper nouns, such as names of people, places, and languages.

Incorrect: today is my birthday.

Correct: Today is my birthday.

Incorrect: I love Horses.

Correct: I love horses.

Practice 1

Read the paragraph. Some sentences are missing capital letters on the first word. Underline the words that should be written with capital letters.

my name is Anush. I am from Armenia. my first language is Armenian. i also speak Russian. Now I live in Los Angeles, California. the city has a large Armenian population. today is the first day of my new English class. I want to speak English well. it is very important for my future. When I finish school, I want to be a veterinarian. it's going to take a long time, but I don't mind. I love animals. my friends say I'm going to be a good vet.

Practice 2

Rewrite each sentence. Add or remove a capital letter if necessary.

Example:

1 *my cousin drives a red sports car.*

     My cousin drives a red sports car.

2 I like to drink Coffee.

_____ .

3 the movie starts at 8:00.

_____ .

4 that's a very sad story.

_____ .

5 John usually studies in the Library.

_____ .

6 are you from Australia?

_____ ?

7 in my family, my father usually cooks dinner.

_____ .

8 The price of Stamps is going up.

_____ .

9 what do you like to do in your free time?

_____ ?

PROPER NOUNS

Presentation

Capital Letters: Proper Nouns

Some nouns begin with capital letters, even in the middle of a sentence. These nouns are called *proper nouns*. Proper nouns are the names of people, places, languages, holidays, and so on.

Here are rules for capitalizing proper nouns.

Rules	Examples
Capitalize the pronoun *I*.	Do you know what **I** want?
Capitalize people's names and titles.	**L**inda **B**arker, **D**r. **B**ruce **F**ogel, **M**s. **C**atherine **L**ee
Capitalize names of cities, states, countries, continents, and streets.	He's from **B**uenos **A**ires, **A**rgentina.
	I live on **H**aines **A**venue.
	The largest continent is **A**sia.
	She lives in **C**olorado.
Capitalize names of languages and nationalities.	He is **E**gyptian.
	He speaks **A**rabic.
Capitalize the days of the week and months of the year.*	**T**uesday, the 12th of **A**ugust
Capitalize names of holidays.	It snowed on **C**hristmas.

*Do not capitalize the seasons: fall, winter, spring, summer

Practice 1

Read the paragraph. Underline eleven words that are proper nouns and need capital letters.

My grandmother is a pediatrician—a doctor for children. Her name is dr. adrienne Rameau. She was born in marseille, in the south of france. She met my grandfather in 1946. He was a soldier in europe. They met on a tuesday and got married one week later. It was november 11, 1946. In the united states, this date is a holiday called veterans day. On this holiday we celebrate the service of all the soldiers in our history.

Practice 2

Rewrite the sentence. Correct all errors with capital letters.

Example:

1 *My birthday is january 18th.*

_____ *My birthday is January 18th.* _____

2 i can meet you on thursday at 6.

_____ .

3 When is your appointment with dr. jackson?

_____ ?

4 My father's office is on orange avenue.

_____ .

5 yolanda is studying chinese.

_____ .

6 The state of alaska has a lot of oil.

_____ .

7 My family moved to cleveland, ohio, on june 15, 2008.

_____ .

8 The largest country in south america is brazil.

_____ .

PARAGRAPH TITLES

Presentation

Capital Letters: Paragraph Titles

Some paragraphs have titles. You should capitalize all the important words in a title.

- Capitalize nouns, pronouns, verbs, adjectives, and adverbs.
- Don't capitalize articles (*a, an, the*) or prepositions (*in, from, at*) unless they are the first word.
- Capitalize only the first letter of important words. Don't capitalize other letters.

Practice 1

Read each title. Then decide whether the title's capitalization is correct or incorrect. For each answer, circle *a* for *Correct* or *b* for *Incorrect*.

Example:

1 *my happiest day*
  a *Correct*
  (b) *Incorrect*

2 a Boring Day
  a Correct
  b Incorrect

3 MY WEDDING DAY
  a Correct
  b Incorrect

4 The Best Job for Me
  a Correct
  b Incorrect

5 How to Listen Carefully
  a Correct
  b Incorrect

6 Introduction To psychology
  a Correct
  b Incorrect

7 the Little Prince
  a Correct
  b Incorrect

8 The Dog In The Window
  a Correct
  b Incorrect

Practice 2

Rewrite each title with correct capitalization.

Example:

1 *around the world in eighty days*

    Around the World in Eighty Days

2 my year in Cairo

_____

3 a serious mistake

_____

4 the health benefits of chocolate

_____

5 AN UNUSUAL JOB

_____

6 it's never too late

_____

7 a perfect pair of boots

_____

8 how to make a perfect cup of coffee

_____

9 one world, many languages

_____

Commas

COMPLEX SENTENCES WITH AFTER, WHEN, BECAUSE, AND IF

Presentation

Complex Sentences with _After, When, Because,_ and _If_

An independent clause is a group of words that can stand on its own as a sentence. A dependent clause cannot stand on its own as a complete sentence. It must be attached to an independent clause. Use a comma after a dependent clause that comes first in a complex sentence. Do not use a comma if the independent clause is first.

Dependent Clauses	Examples
With _after_	After Josh finished high school, he joined the army.
	Josh joined the army after he finished high school.
With _when_	When it rains, there are bad traffic jams.
	There are bad traffic jams when it rains.
With _because_	Because she speaks Chinese, Julie got a good job.
	Julie got a good job because she speaks Chinese.
With _if_	If you wait half an hour, I will drive you home.
	I will drive you home if you wait half an hour.

Practice 1

Read each sentence. Circle *Correct* if the comma is used correctly. Circle *Incorrect* if it is not.

Example:

1 *I admire my father, because he is kind and honest.*
   a *Correct*
   ⓑ *Incorrect*

2 After the guests left, I washed the dishes.
   a Correct
   b Incorrect

3 I will buy a car, if I get a good job.
   a Correct
   b Incorrect

4 Because you helped me I passed my exam.
   a Correct
   b Incorrect

5 I will go to the bank, when it stops raining.
   a Correct
   b Incorrect

6 If I feel better tomorrow, I will go to the gym.
   a Correct
   b Incorrect

7 I stopped reading the book, because it was boring.
   b Correct
   b Incorrect

8 After they got married, Jack and Jill bought a house.
   a Correct
   b Incorrect

9 When the concert ended the audience clapped for five minutes.
   a Correct
   b Incorrect

Practice 2

Circle the letter of the correct sentence in each group.

1 a Please wash the dog before you go out.
   b Please wash the dog, before you go out.
   c Please wash the dog before, you go out.

2 a The Hari family moved to Seattle, because Mrs. Hari got a job there.
   b The Hari family moved to Seattle because Mrs. Hari got a job there.
   c The Hari family moved to Seattle because, Mrs. Hari got a job there.

3 a After he had a heart attack Mr. Chao lost 20 pounds.
   b After he had a heart attack, Mr. Chao lost 20 pounds.
   c After, he had a heart attack Mr. Chao lost 20 pounds.

4 a Be sure to close the windows, when you leave.
   b Be sure to close the windows when, you leave.
   c Be sure to close the windows when you leave.

5 **a** Because she is very tall, Carla is uncomfortable on airplanes.
   b Because she is very tall Carla is uncomfortable on airplanes.
   c Because, she is very tall Carla, is uncomfortable on airplanes.

6 **a** I felt very sad after, the movie ended.
   b I felt very sad, after the movie ended.
   c I felt very sad after the movie ended.

7 **a** It's polite to say "Excuse me" if you burp.
   b It's polite, to say "Excuse me" if you burp.
   c It's polite to say "Excuse me," if you burp.

8 **a** When their pet dies many people become depressed.
   b When their pet dies many people, become depressed.
   c When their pet dies, many people become depressed.

9 **a** If I make a mistake I try to fix it.
   b If I make a mistake, I try to fix it.
   c If I make a mistake I try, to fix it.

COMPOUND SENTENCES WITH AND, BUT, SO, AND OR

Presentation

Commas in Compound Sentences with *And, But, So,* and *Or*

Compound sentences are two independent clauses that are joined together. *And, or, but,* and *so* are called conjunctions. They combine two independent clauses. Use a comma before *and, or, but,* and *so* in compound sentences.

Examples:

Judy became a vegetarian, **and** she lost 15 pounds.

George wants to go home, **but** his wife wants to stay at the party.

Carol is 6 feet tall, **so** it is hard for her to find women's clothes that fit.

Ben will go to law school, **or** he will get a job at his father's company.

Don't use a comma in simple sentences with one subject and two verbs.

Incorrect: I read the paper, and walked the dog before work.

Correct: I read the paper and walked the dog before work.

Practice 1

Read the sentences. If commas are used correctly, circle *a* for *Correct*. If commas are used incorrectly, circle *b* for *Incorrect*.

1 Regina sings, and plays guitar in a rock band.
   a Correct
   b Incorrect

2 My office is downtown so I take the bus to work.
   a Correct
   b Incorrect

3 I have a dog, and my roommate has two cats.
  a Correct
  b Incorrect

4 On weekends, Nancy often goes to museums or visits friends.
  a Correct
  b Incorrect

5 I need to study harder, or I will not pass my chemistry class.
  a Correct
  b Incorrect

6 David's apartment is tiny and, the rent is high.
  b Correct
  b Incorrect

7 Min's family lives far away so he feels lonely sometimes.
  a Correct
  b Incorrect

8 Los Angeles is full of people but it's not easy to make friends.
  a Correct
  b Incorrect

Practice 2

Combine each pair of simple sentences into a compound sentence. Use the conjunction in parentheses and a comma.

Example:

1 *(and) I'm tired. I want to go home.*

   I'm <u>tired, and I want to</u> go home.

2 (and) My son is six years old. My daughter is three.

   My son is six _____ is three.

3 (but) I studied hard. I failed the exam.

   I _____ the exam.

4 (so) It's late. I need to leave.

   It's _____ to leave.

5 (or) I'll have lunch now. I'll eat after the meeting.

   I'll _____ after the meeting.

6 (so) The dress was the wrong color. I returned it.

   The dress was _____ I returned it.

7 (and) The book was long. It was hard to understand.

   The book _____ to understand.

8 (but) We went to the mall. We didn't buy anything.

   We went _____ anything.

9 (or) The groom will wear a tuxedo. He'll wear a dark suit.

   The groom will _____ wear a dark suit.

PUNCTUATING DATES

Punctuating Dates

Rules	Examples
Use a comma between the day and the year.	January 18, 1978
Use a comma after a date in a sentence.	June 12, 1988, was Ben's graduation day.
Do not use a comma with a year alone.	I was born in 1985.
Do not use a comma in a date with *of*.	We visited Tokyo in March of 2008.

Practice 1

Rewrite the date. Use commas correctly.

1 January 1 2010

_____

2 February 12 1986

_____

3 July 4 1776

_____

4 December 25 1945

_____

5 April 12 2004

_____

6 October 31 1999

_____

7 September 3 1919

_____

8 July 14 1789

_____

Practice 2

Are commas used correctly in the following sentences? Circle *a* for *Correct* or *b* for *Incorrect*.

Example:

1 *I was born on May 15 1988.*
   a *Correct*
   (b) *Incorrect*

2 The United States became an independent country in 1776.
   a Correct
   b Incorrect

3 January 23, 2008 was the day John's life changed forever.
   a Correct
   b Incorrect

4 Ellen's first child was born in 2004.
   a Correct
   b Incorrect

5 In November, of 2014 Frank will turn 21.
   a Correct
   b Incorrect

6 Francine will graduate from medical school on June 15 2015.
   a Correct
   b Incorrect

7 In September of 2008 my family had a big reunion.
   a Correct
   b Incorrect

8 May 3, 2001, was Bianca's first day at her job.
   a Correct
   b Incorrect

9 Mark will have knee surgery on August 3, 2014.
   a Correct
   b Incorrect

ITEMS IN A SERIES

Presentation

Commas: Items in a Series

A *series* is a list of three or more items. The list can include words or phrases. Use commas between the items in a series. Use *and* or *or* before the last item. Use a comma before *and* or *or*.

Do not use a comma to connect only two items.

Examples:

   Correct: We need milk, bread, apples, and eggs.

   Incorrect: We need milk, and bread.

Practice 1

Are commas used correctly in the following sentences? Circle the letter for _Correct_ or _Incorrect_ in each answer.

1 My favorite fruits are apples, oranges, and strawberries.
  a Correct
  b Incorrect

2 The American flag is red white and blue.
  a Correct
  b Incorrect

3 Marco, Jin-So, and Kayako are in one group.
  a Correct
  b Incorrect

4 December, and January are the coldest months.
  a Correct
  b Incorrect

5 You can wear the boots with pants, skirts or dresses.
  a Correct
  b Incorrect

6 Before work I always read the newspaper, check my email, walk the dog, and call my mother.
  a Correct
  b Incorrect

7 The airline offers free coffee, tea, milk, and soft drinks.
  a Correct
  b Incorrect

8 You can download the program to your phone, or computer.
  a Correct
  b Incorrect

Practice 2

Rewrite the list. Use commas correctly.

Example:

1 _We plan to visit Prague Vienna and Budapest._
  _____We plan to visit Prague, Vienna, and Budapest._____

2 There are trees grass and flowers in my garden.
  There are _____ in my garden.

3 On Monday Tuesday and Wednesday, Juan works from 8:00 to 5:00.
  On _____ , Juan works from 8:00 to 5:00.

4 My grandparents uncles aunts and cousins attended my college graduation.
  My _____ attended my college graduation.

5 Would you like tea coffee or juice with your breakfast?
  Would you like _____ with your breakfast?

6 Information for voters is available in English Spanish French German Polish and Italian.

Information for voters is available in _____ .

7 Grandma doesn't like salty sweet or spicy foods.

Grandma doesn't like _____ foods.

8 Gregory's hobbies are reading swimming and playing guitar.

Gregory's hobbies are _____ .

9 Mike Sara Thomas or Ahmed will be your partner.

_____ will be your partner.

TIME SIGNALS

Presentation

Commas: Time Signals

- Use a comma after a time expression, time-order word, or prepositional phrase of time at the beginning of a sentence.
- Do not use a comma after *then*.
- Do not use a comma before a time signal at the end of a sentence.

Time Signals	Examples
Time expressions	**Once a month,** my friends and I get together for an evening of fun.
	Last night, we had a great time.
Time-order words	**First,** we had dinner at an Indian restaurant.
	Then we went to a movie.
	Later, we went dancing at a club downtown.
Prepositional phrases	**In 2005,** I studied in Spain.
	After dinner, we took a walk.
	We went to Barcelona **in December**.

Practice 1

Read the sentence. Are commas used correctly? Circle the letter for *Correct* or *Incorrect*.

Example:

1 *Once a year I visit my grandparents in Quebec.*
  a *Correct*   **(b)** *Incorrect*

2 Carmen cleans her kitchen once a week.
  a Correct   **b** Incorrect

3 First, she sweeps the floor.
  a Correct   **b** Incorrect

4 Then, she checks the refrigerator for old food and throws it away.
  a Correct   **b** Incorrect

5 After that, she cleans the sink and the counters.
  a Correct   **b** Incorrect

6 Next she washes the floor.
  a Correct   **b** Incorrect

7 She waits 15 minutes for the floor to dry.
  a Correct   **b** Incorrect

8 Finally, she takes out the garbage.
  a Correct   **b** Incorrect

9 Once a month she polishes the floor.
  a Correct   **b** Incorrect

Practice 2

Read the sentences. Circle the letter of the sentence that uses commas correctly.

1 a Yesterday morning I woke up, very early.
  b Yesterday morning, I woke up very early.

2 a Last January Dr. Brenner, took several trips.
  b Last January, Dr. Brenner took several trips.

3 a On January 5th, he flew to New York for a meeting.
  b On January 5th he flew to New York, for a meeting.

4 a After the meeting, he traveled to Boston to visit his son.
  b After the meeting he traveled, to Boston to visit his son.

5 a Two days later, he took the train to Toronto.
  b Two days later he took the train to, Toronto.

6 a The next, morning he spoke at a conference.
  b The next morning, he spoke at a conference.

7 a After the conference, he traveled to Montreal to visit friends.
  b After the conference he traveled to Montreal to, visit friends.

8 a During his, visit the weather was very cold.
  b During his visit, the weather was very cold.

9 a Finally, he flew home to San Francisco on January 16th.
  b Finally he flew home to San Francisco, on January 16th.

End Punctuation

Presentation

End Punctuation: Period, Question Mark, Exclamation Point

Every English sentence has a punctuation mark at the end. A sentence can end with a period, a question mark, or an exclamation point.

Rules	Examples
Most sentences end with a period. They are statements.	Let's go for a walk.
Use a question mark at the end of questions.	How are you today?
	Where is the elevator?
Use an exclamation point to show strong feelings, such as surprise, excitement, or anger.	I can't believe it!
	I hated that movie!

Practice 1

Insert a period, question mark, or exclamation point at the end of each sentence. Some sentences may have more than one correct answer.

Example:

1 *My name is Anush* _____._____

2 Last week I went to the art museum _____

3 I saw the exhibit of paintings by Salvador Dali _____

4 It was incredible _____

5 Do you like modern art _____

6 Last Saturday was my 30th birthday _____

7 My wife wanted to surprise me _____

8 What do you think she did _____

9 First, she cooked my favorite breakfast _____

10 Then she told me she was pregnant _____

11 That was an amazing birthday present _____

Practice 2

Write the sentence or question in the correct order. Then add a period, exclamation point, or question mark.

Example:

1 *name / My / Anush / is*

               My name is Anush.

2 doughnuts / you / like / Do

_____

3 round / are / Doughnuts / cakes

_____

4 a / middle / They / hole / have / the / in

_____

5 American / food / Doughnuts / my / are / favorite

_____

6 they / delicious / are / think / I

_____

7 Look / dog / that / big / at

_____

8 dog / What / it / is / kind / of

_____

9 Great / Dane / is / It / a

_____

10 much / weigh / How / it / does

_____

11 gentle / Danes / are / very / Great

_____

Paragraph Format

Presentation

Paragraph Format

Paragraphs in English have a special *format*—that is, the way a paragraph looks on the page. Follow these guidelines.

- Include a **heading** at the top of the page on the left-hand side. The heading includes your name, the date, and the course number.

- In an academic paragraph, write a **title** on the top line in the middle. The title tells the reader what the paragraph is about.

- Leave spaces on the top, on the bottom, on the left side, and on the right side of your page. These spaces are called **margins**. The left-side margin should be straight. The right-side margin does not need to be straight.

- **Indent** the first line of the paragraph. This means you start writing five spaces from the left margin.

- Begin each sentence with a capital letter.

- End each sentence with **punctuation**—a period, a question mark, or an exclamation point.

- When you finish a sentence, continue writing on the same line. Don't write each sentence on a separate line.

- Leave one space between the end of one sentence and the beginning of the next sentence.

- Leave a blank space between lines. This is called **double-spacing**.

- Do not divide words at the end of a line. Move the whole word to the next line.

Practice 1

Example:

Katya Belov
English 100
November 20, 2013

The Amazing Cockroach

Cockroaches have lived on Earth for more than 400 million years. Three characteristics explain this insect's amazing ability to survive. First of all, cockroaches can live almost anywhere—outdoors in tropical climates and indoors in cooler ones. They prefer warm, humid places. For that reason, they are often found in homes and factories where food is prepared and stored. Another characteristic that helps cockroaches survive is that they will eat almost anything. Their diet includes not only human food but also dead insects, paper, and even glue! Finally, cockroaches have few natural enemies. They smell bad, and eating them causes most birds and animals to get sick. These three reasons explain why cockroaches will probably survive on Earth long after most other animals disappear.

Circle the letter of the correct answer.

1 If a word is too long to fit on a line, you should _____ .
  a move the word to the next line
  b divide the word into smaller parts
  c check the spelling of the word
  d use a smaller word

2 A paragraph heading should be _____ .
  a at the top center and single-spaced
  b at the top left and single-spaced
  c at the top center and double-spaced
  d at the top left and double-spaced

3 The paragraph title should be _____ .
  a the last sentence of the paragraph
  b the first sentence of the paragraph
  c just above the paragraph and centered
  d just above the heading and centered

4 The left-side margins of a paragraph should be _____ .
  a the same as the right-side margins
  b straight
  c indented
  d none of the above

5 The first line of a paragraph should be _____ .
  a in all capital letters
  b double-spaced
  c in bold
  d indented

Practice 2

Read the paragraph. Is it formatted correctly or incorrectly? Circle the letter of *Correct* **or** *Incorrect*.

Marianne Sanders
November 23, 2013

No Pets on Board

Some people bring dogs and cats on airplanes. I don't like this for several reasons.

First, some people are allergic to animals. If they are sitting near a dog or cat, they can get sick.

Second, animals can make noise. This can disturb passengers who want to read, sleep, or relax.   Third, I think it is cruel to bring animals

on long flights. They need   to be in a cage all the time, and maybe they will be scared. Some owners are not   responsible, and they take their pet out of the cage. Then the pet can escape, and the flight attendants have to catch them. This is unsafe. For these reasons, I don't think people should

bring their pets on airplanes.

1 Heading
  a Correct
  b Incorrect

2 Title
  a Correct
  b Incorrect

3 Capital letters
  a Correct
  b Incorrect

4 Final punctuation
  a Correct
  b Incorrect

5 Double-spacing
  a Correct
  b Incorrect

6 Indentation
  a Correct
  b Incorrect

7 Left margin
  a Correct
  b Incorrect

8 Right margin
  a Correct
  b Incorrect

9 Space between sentences
  a Correct
  b Incorrect

Spelling

THIRD-PERSON SINGULAR -*S*

Presentation

Spelling: Third-Person Singular -*s*

We use the third-person singular present tense to talk about people or things in the singular form. The pronouns for the third-person singular are *he, she,* and *it.* The present tense describes things that happen in the present or that are habitual.

Examples:

Jamila watches TV every night.

He has a lot of money.

Rules	Examples
Add -*s* to form the third-person singular of most present singular verbs.	walk > walks
Add -*es* to verbs ending in -*s*, -*z*, -*x*, -*sh*, and -*ch*.	kiss > kisses
	buzz > buzzes
	fix > fixes
	push > pushes
	watch > watches
If a verb ends in consonant + -*y*, change the *y* to *i* and add -*es*.	try > tries
If a verb ends in vowel + -*y*, do not change the ending.	pay > pays
Have, be, and *do* have irregular third-person singular forms.	be > is
	do > does
	have > has

Practice 1

Circle the letter of the word that uses the third-person singular correctly.

Example:

1 *walk*

   a *walkes*

   (b) *walks*

2 do

   a does

   b dos

3 eat

   a eates

   b eats

4 teach

   a teaches

   b teachs

5 cry

   a cries

   b crys

6 play

   a plaies

   b plays

7 have

   a has

   b haves

8 buy

   a buyes

   b buys

9 carry

   a carries

   b carrys

10 see

   a sees

   b seez

11 wash

   a washes

   b washs

12 try

   a tries

   b trys

Practice 2

Write the third-person singular form of each verb.

Example:

1 *speak*: _____*speaks*_____

2 write: _____

3 study: _____

4 pay: _____

5 watch: _____

6 fly: _____

7 go: _____

8 read: _____

9 brush: _____

10 fix: _____

11 pass: _____

-ING

Presentation

Spelling: *-ing*

Use the *-ing* ending to form the present progressive of verbs. The present progressive is used to describe actions that are happening at the moment of speaking or that are temporary.

Examples:

I am running to the store right now.

My mother is living in Spain for a month.

Rules	Examples
Add *-ing* to the base form of most verbs.	walk > walking
	read > reading
If a verb ends in -e, drop the e and add *-ing*.	come > coming
If a one-syllable verb ends in consonant + vowel + consonant (CVC), then double the last consonant and add *-ing*.	sit > sitting
Do not double the last consonant if a word ends in *w*, *x*, or *y*.	flow > flowing
	fix > fixing
	play > playing

Practice 1

Circle the letter of the answer with the correct spelling.

Example:

1 *run:*
  a *runing*
  (b) *running*

2 take:
  a taking
  b takking

3 happen:
  a happening
  b happenning

4 wait:
  a waiting
  b waitting

5 grow:

   a growing

   b growwing

6 study:

   a studing

   b studying

7 hit:

   a hiting

   b hitting

8 bite:

   a biting

   b bitting

9 plan:

   a planing

   b planning

10 sleep:

   a sleeping

   b sleepping

11 stop:

   a stoping

   b stopping

Practice 2

Write the *-ing* form of each verb.

Example:

1 *speak:* _____speaking_____

2 write: _____

3 study: _____

4 clap: _____

5 cry: _____

6 blow: _____

7 go: _____

8 cut: _____

9 smile: _____

10 rain: _____

11 pass: _____

REGULAR PAST-TENSE VERBS

Presentation

Spelling: Regular Past-Tense Verbs

Use the *-ed* ending to form the past tense of regular verbs.

Rules	Examples
If a verb ends in a consonant, add *-ed*.	jump > jumped
If a verb ends in -e, add *-d*.	like > liked
If a verb ends in consonant + -y, change the y to i and add *-ed*.	carry > carried
If the verb ends in vowel + -y, do not change the y to i. Just add *-ed*.	play > played
If a one-syllable verb ends in consonant + vowel + consonant (CVC), then double the last consonant and add *-ed*.	jog > jogged
Do not double the last consonant if a word ends in w, x, or y.	fix > fixed

Practice 1

Circle the letter of the word with the correct spelling.

Example:

1 *like:*
   (a) *liked*
   b *likeed*

2 cook:
   a cooked
   b cookked

3 smile:
   a smild
   b smiled

4 enjoy:
   a enjoyed
   b enjoyyed

5 hurry:
   a hurried
   b hurryed

6 plan:
   a planed
   b planned

7 relax:
   a relaxed
   b relaxxed

8 snow:
   a snowed
   b snowwed

9 clean:
   a cleaned
   b cleanned

10 study:
   a studied
   b studyed

11 dance:
   a danced
   b dancied

Practice 2

Write the regular past-tense form of each verb.

Example:

1 *clean:* _____cleaned_____

2 watch: _____

3 study: _____

4 clap: _____

5 cry: _____

6 allow: _____

7 tax: _____

8 carry: _____

9 shave: _____

10 rain: _____

11 pass: _____

GRAMMAR

Articles

ARTICLES A AND AN

Presentation

Articles *A* and *An*

A and *an* are indefinite articles. Articles often come before nouns.

Rules	Examples
Use *a* before a consonant sound.	a boy, a classroom, a horse, a university*
Use *an* before a vowel sound.	an animal, an egg, an hour**
Use *a* and *an* before singular count nouns. Count nouns are nouns that can be counted; they have a singular and plural form.	a cup, an umbrella
Do not use *a* and *an* before noncount nouns or plural nouns. Noncount nouns can't be counted; they don't have a plural form.	<u>Incorrect:</u> I want a water. (noncount noun) <u>Correct:</u> I want water.
	<u>Incorrect:</u> She usually wears a boots. (plural noun) <u>Correct:</u> She usually wears boots.
Adjectives come between articles and singular nouns.	a new car, an old boot

* The first sound is /ū/, as in *you*.
** The *h* is silent. The first sound is a vowel.

Practice 1

Circle *a*, *an*, or *X* (no article).

1 Budapest is [a, an, X] city.

2 Sam is eating [an, a, X] apple.

3 I have [an, a, X] idea.

4 I have [a, an, X] strange idea.

5 That store sells [X, a, an] bicycles.

6 I asked my parents to send me [X, a, an] money.

7 I will see you in [an, a, X] hour.

8 That's [a, an, X] happy baby.

9 Last night we went to [a, an, X] concert.

10 Would you like [an, a, X] omelette for lunch?

Practice 2

Fill in the blank with *a*, *an*, or *X* (no article).

Example:

1 *I have a new car.*

2 There is _____ university in my town.

3 Gabriel is allergic to _____ eggs.

4 The pants are _____ inch too short.

5 Alicia needs _____ glasses.

6 My grandmother sent me _____ check.

7 Don't forget to take _____ umbrella.

8 I want to tell you _____ joke.

9 Most people hate _____ snakes.

10 Carla has _____ red sports car.

11 Indira bought _____ expensive computer.

A VS. THE

Presentation

A vs. The

A and *an* are indefinite articles. *The* is a definite article. Use *the* to refer to definite, specific objects. *A* or *an* are for indefinite, non-specific objects.

Rules	Examples
Use *the* with singular count nouns, plural nouns, and noncount nouns.	the park, the houses, the water
Use *the* before specific things that both the speaker and listener know about.	Not specific: Melons contain vitamin C. (*Melons* means all melons or melons in general. No article.)
	Specific: **The** melons at that store are delicious. (Specific melons at a specific store.)
	Not specific: There's a supermarket in my neighborhood. (In this sentence, *a* means *one*.)
	Specific: I'm going to **the** supermarket. Do you want anything? (In this sentence, both the speaker and the listener know which supermarket the speaker means.)
Use *the* when there is only one of something.	the sun, the day after tomorrow, the president
Use *the* when you repeat a noun you already talked about.	Yesterday I bought a used car. **The** car had only 15,000 miles.

Practice 1

Circle the correct article to complete the sentence.

1 We live in [an, the] old house in [a, the] beautiful neighborhood. [The, A] house was built in 1928.

2 Anwar is from Riyadh. Riyadh is [the, a] capital of Saudi Arabia.

3 Anna: Robert, can you please pick up my medicine at [the, a] drugstore after work? Robert: Sure, no problem.

4 Lee has [a, the] part-time job at [a, the] newest gas station. Lee likes [the, a] people who work with him. They are friendly.

5 [The, A] weather is terrible today. It's snowing, and it's very cold.

6 A: I'm hungry.
B: Would you like [an, the] apple?

A and *an* are indefinite articles. *The* is a definite article. Use *the* to refer to definite, specific objects. *A* or *an* are for indefinite, non-specific objects.

Rules	Examples
Use *the* with singular count nouns, plural nouns, and noncount nouns.	the park, the houses, the water
Use *the* before specific things that both the speaker and listener know about.	<u>Not specific:</u> Melons contain vitamin C. (*Melons* means all melons or melons in general. No article.)
	<u>Specific:</u> **The** melons at that store are delicious. (Specific melons at a specific store.)
	<u>Not specific:</u> There's a supermarket in my neighborhood. (In this sentence, *a* means *one*.)
	<u>Specific:</u> I'm going to **the** supermarket. Do you want anything? (In this sentence, both the speaker and the listener know which supermarket the speaker means.)
Use *the* when there is only one of something.	the sun, the day after tomorrow, the president
Use *the* when you repeat a noun you already talked about.	Yesterday I bought a used car. **The** car had only 15,000 miles.

Practice 2

Complete the sentence with *a*, *an*, or *the*.

1 A: We have _____ new baby in our family.

   B: Congratulations!

2 A: Are you going to _____ bank today?

   B: Yes. I'm going to deposit my paycheck.

3 A: Could you please pass _____ salt?

   B: Here you go.

4 A: They're going to build _____ biggest new airport near our town.

   B: That's good. _____ old airport is too small.

5 A: I need _____ vacation.

   B: Where would you like to go?

6 A: I love _____ furniture in this room.

B: Thank you. We like it, too.

7 A: Where are you from?

B: Reykjavik. It's _____ capital of Iceland.

8 A: Where are _____ car keys?

B: In my purse.

9 A: What happened to _____ ice cream I bought last week?

B: We finished it last night. Don't you remember?

Adjectives

ADJECTIVES WITH BE

Presentation	
Adjectives with *Be*	
Adjectives describe nouns. You can use them in several ways.	

Rules	Examples
Adjectives can come after all forms of the verb *be*.	I am **tired**.
	You are **funny**.
	He/ She / It is **interesting**.
	We / They are **tall**.
You can connect adjectives with *and*.	Karina is **nice** and **polite**.
Do not add –s to adjectives in English.	<u>Incorrect:</u> The shoes are olds.
	<u>Correct:</u> The shoes are old.
Place adverbs before adjectives.	She is **very** smart.

Practice 1

Read the paragraph. Circle ten adjectives.

My sister's name is Ellen Baker. I think she is very pretty. Her hair is short and blond, and her eyes are blue. She is short, and she is very thin. One thing about Ellen is very special. She has lots of freckles, especially on her nose. They're really cute! Ellen has very light skin, so she's always careful in the sun.

Practice 2

Read the sentence. Are the adjectives used correctly? Underline *Correct* or *Incorrect*.

Example:

1 *These houses are olds.*
Correct
<u>Incorrect</u>

2 After a long day at work, Hila is tired.
Correct
Incorrect

3 That shirt is too small for you.
Correct
Incorrect

4 The cat's eyes are greens.
Correct
Incorrect

5 The roses in my neighbor's garden are beautifuls.
Correct
Incorrect

6 This apple juice is cold and delicious.
Correct
Incorrect

7 My classmate Angel tall is.
Correct
Incorrect

8 The elevator is full.
Correct
Incorrect

9 My mother's advice is usually correct.
Correct
Incorrect

10 Your ideas very interesting are.
Correct
Incorrect

11 The textbooks for my history class are very expensives.
Correct
Incorrect

ADJECTIVE ORDER

Adjective Order

- Adjectives can come before nouns (e.g., a **big** house) or after *be* (e.g., The house is **big**.).

- There can be more than one adjective before a noun; for example, *five old Italian coins*. Adjectives usually go in this order:

Note: If two or more adjectives from the same category are in a row, separate them with commas: *a red, white, and blue flag* (colors); *an unfriendly, mean cat* (opinion).

Categories	Examples
Quantity	two, some, many
Size	short, large
Opinion / Condition	beautiful, broken
Physical description (shape, age, color)	square, old, blue
Origin	American, African, Indian
Material	wood, glass
Noun used as adjective	coffee (cup), wedding (dress)

Practice 1

Read the sentence. Are the adjectives in the correct order? Circle *Correct* or *Incorrect*.

Example:

1 *a beautiful old apartment building*
Correct
Incorrect

2 She drives an old big American car.
Correct
Incorrect

3 Tzatziki is a creamy yogurt sauce from Greece.
Correct
Incorrect

4 I bought an Indian colorful bedspread.

Correct

Incorrect

5 My neighbor is a Canadian sad old lady.

Correct

Incorrect

6 John gave his wife a bouquet of beautiful red roses.

Correct

Incorrect

7 I don't like those plastic uncomfortable chairs.

Correct

Incorrect

8 My parents have a black, small, noisy dog.

Correct

Incorrect

9 For dessert we had a delicious chocolate cake.

Correct

Incorrect

10 The house has three large bedrooms.

Correct

Incorrect

11 There are several glass large lamps in the hall.

Correct

Incorrect

Practice 2

Write the adjectives in the correct order.

Example:

1

Greek	traditional

My cousin had a _traditional Greek_ wedding.

2

white	beautiful	silk

She wore a _____ _____ _____ wedding dress.

3

long	lace

The dress had a _____ _____ train.

4

Greek	large

The groom also comes from a _____ _____ family.

5

formal	gray

He wore a _____ _____ suit.

6

many	wonderful	wedding

My cousin received _____ _____ _____ gifts.

7

antique	tall	silver

Her favorite gift was a pair of _____ _____ _____ candlesticks.

8

beautiful	six	rose

There are _____ _____ _____ bushes in our front yard.

9

glass	coffee	square

We have a _____ _____ _____ table.

10

small	three

Mr. and Mrs. Green have _____ _____ children.

POSSESSIVE ADJECTIVES

Presentation

Possessive Adjectives

Possessive adjectives come before nouns. They show that something belongs to somebody or something.

Possessive Adjectives	Examples
my	That's **my** book.
your (singular and plural)	I like **your** brother.
his, her, its	**His** computer is slow.
our	**Our** furniture is old.
their	I don't know **their** address.

Practice 1

Circle the possessive adjective in each sentence.

1 I can't find my watch.

2 Mina started her first job last week.

3 I can't remember where I parked my car.

4 Our new neighbors aren't very friendly.

5 Can I borrow your phone?

6 She had a baby boy last week. His name is Kevin.

7 Ron and Sue usually visit their grandmother on Sunday afternoon.

8 Please send me an email with a link to your website.

9 Edward's mother is a doctor, and his father is a nurse.

10 That island is famous for its beautiful beaches and wonderful weather.

11 We finally cleaned our apartment.

Practice 2

Complete each sentence with the correct possessive adjective.

Example:

I can't find <u>my</u> watch.

1 I enjoy spending time with _____ cousins.

2 Susannah's little sister loves _____ new doll.

3 It's normal for parents to love _____ children.

4 Daniel uses _____ phone to communicate with friends.

5 Every country has _____ special foods.

6 My wife and I love _____ new house.

7 How many people are in _____ family, Benny?

8 The Johnsons sold _____ house.

9 Is that _____ car, Rachel? It's beautiful.

10 My roommate and I hope you can come to _____ party.

Nouns

PLURAL COUNT NOUNS

Presentation

Plural Count Nouns

Count nouns are separate things. You can count them (*one ball, two balls*).

Count nouns have two forms: singular and plural. We use *a/an* before singular count nouns. Plural count nouns have different forms.

See Appendix 11 for complete spelling rules.

Rules	Examples
For most plural count nouns, add -*s*.	shirts, telephones, computers
For plural count nouns ending in *x*, *ch*, *sh*, or *ss*, add -*es*.	boxes, watches, stashes, classes
Some plural count nouns are irregular.	child > children, man > men, woman > women, tooth > teeth, foot > feet
Some count nouns have the same form in the singular and plural.	fish, sheep

Practice 1

Underline the plural nouns in the shopping list.

matches

milk

a pineapple

potatoes

bread

toothpaste

eggs

paper towels

a chicken

Practice 2

Complete the sentence. Use the plural form of a word from the list.

costume	chair	child
glass	box	foot
name	tooth	sister
fish	American	

Example:

1 I'm the oldest sibling in my family. I have two younger *sisters*.

2 Bob drank two _____ of water.

3 These _____ are very comfortable.

4 The _____ are learning how to hold a pencil.

5 I enjoy looking at the _____ in the aquarium.

6 My _____ hurt after walking all day.

7 On Halloween, we enjoy dressing up in _____ .

8 Many _____ are choosing to eat less meat.

9 Don't forget to brush your _____ before bed.

10 I'm moving, so I'm putting all my things in _____ .

11 Mrs. Kelly can't remember her students' _____ .

NONCOUNT NOUNS

Presentation

Noncount Nouns

Count nouns are things we can count. For example, we can say "one class" or "two classes." Noncount nouns are things we cannot count. Noncount nouns do not have a plural form. They take singular verbs. They do not use *a/an*. You can use quantity words (*some, any, a lot of, some*) with them to express an amount.

Example:

Correct: I don't like homework. / We don't have any homework.

Incorrect: The teacher gave us a homework. / Tonight I have three homeworks.

It is helpful to learn noncount nouns in categories:

Categories	Examples
food	bread, ice cream, butter, salt, cheese, sugar
liquids	milk, soda, beer, juice, gasoline
school subjects	chemistry, English, history
ideas	love, anger, happiness, time, help
things in nature	oxygen, air, light
other common words	furniture, information, software, money, music

Practice 1

Underline the correct answer to complete each sentence.

Example:

1 *Please give me* [a, <u>an</u>] *apple.*

2 Jennifer is studying [X, a] psychology.

3 I don't have [any, a] homework tonight.

4 Jonah is looking for [a, X] job.

5 Hannah doesn't like [X, a] cheese.

6 Do you want [any, a] help?

7 I'm sorry. I don't have [X, a] time to help you.

8 It takes [an, X] hour to drive to the lake.

9 I need [X, a] good luck on my final exam.

10 I need to put [some, a] gas in the car.

11 Plants need [X, a] light to grow.

Practice 2

Underline the word or phrase that correctly completes each sentence.

Example:

1 *I usually don't put* [salt, a salt] in my soup.

2 Do you have [information, informations] about the train schedule?

3 I will buy [bread, a bread] this afternoon.

4 I am looking for [help, a help].

5 Sandra does not drink [alcohol, alcohols].

6 I need to get [money, a money] at the bank.

7 Zina doesn't like rap [music, musics].

8 Babies drink [milk, milks].

9 I don't like [fast food, a fast food]. It isn't healthy.

10 It is boring to sit in [traffic, a traffic].

11 They eat [rice, rices] every day.

Future

FUTURE WITH BE GOING TO

Presentation

Future with *Be Going To*

Be going to + verb is one way of expressing the future in English.

Be going to:

- Make sure that the form of *be* (*am*, *is*, *are*) agrees with the subject.
- To form the negative, put *not* after be.
- You can use contractions with *be going to*: *I'm / You're / He's / She's / It's / We're / They're going to*.

Forms	Examples
Affirmative statements	I **am going to** buy a new car.
	You / we / they **are / 're going to** be late.
	He /she / it **is / 's going to** come.
Negative statements	I **am not / I'm not going to** graduate.
	You / we / they **are not / 're not / aren't going to** come.
	He / she / it **is not / 's not / isn't going to** come.
Yes/No questions	**Am I going to** be late?
	Are you / we / they **going to** take the bus?
	Is he / she it **going to** come?
Wh- questions	Where **am I going to** live?
	When **are** you / we / they **going to** leave?
	Who **is** he / she / it **going to** meet?

Meanings of *be going to*

Meanings	Examples
Future plans	Paul **is going to** graduate in June.
Predictions or guesses	It**'s going to** rain. Jackson **is going to** be tall like his father.

Practice 1

Underline the correct form to complete each sentence.

Example:

We [are going to have, going to have] visitors next week.

A: Next week my cousin and her family [are going to, going to] come to Los Angeles.

B: What [are they going to do, they going to do] here?

A: They ['re going to go, going to go] to Hollywood on Monday.

B: [Are you going to go, You going to go] with them?

A: No, I [am going to stay, going to stay] home that day. But on Tuesday, we ['re going to go, going to go] to the beach together.

B: What about your wife? [Is she going to, She is going to] join you?

A: Yes, [she's going to, she going to] take the day off from work.

B: It sounds like [it's going to be, it be] fun.

A: Definitely. And we can eat in restaurants. [I'm not going to cook, I'm not go cooking]!

Practice 2

Complete each sentence with the correct form of *be going to*. Use the verb in parentheses.

Example:

It *'s going to rain* (rain).

A: Next month, my family _____ (have) a family reunion in my hometown.

B: That's sounds like fun. Who _____ (attend)?

A: My grandparents and most of their children and grandchildren. But unfortunately my brother _____ (not attend) because he is in the army.

B: Where _____ (you / stay)?

A: I _____ (stay) with my cousin Betsy.

B: _____ (your parents / stay) there, too?

A: No. They _____ (stay) at a hotel.

B: I'm sure the reunion _____ (be) lots of fun.

A: Oh yeah. We _____ (eat), talk, play games, tell stories, and spend time outdoors if the weather is nice. And I _____ (not worry) about anything.

FUTURE WITH WILL

Presentation

Future with *Will*

Use *will* + verb to talk about the future.

- The form is the same for all persons: *will* + verb
- To form the negative, put *not* after *will*.
- You can use contracted forms with *will*:

Affirmative: *I'll, you'll, he'll, she'll, it'll, we'll, they'll*

Negative: *I / you / he / she / it / we / they won't*

Forms	Examples
Affirmative statements	I **will** / **I'll** see you later.
	They **will** / They**'ll** do a great job.
Negative statements	You **will not** / **won't** believe it.
	We **will not** / **won't** be late.
Yes/No questions	**Will** she be there?
	Will they have time?
Wh- questions	Where **will** you be?
	When **will** we meet?

Meanings	Examples
Future events*	This year, I **will** graduate from college.
Predictions or guesses*	We **will** arrive at 6:00.
Promises or offers	I **will** help you.
*You can also use *be going to* + verb for these meanings.	

Practice 1

Underline the correct form to complete each sentence.

Example:

1 We <u>will have</u> visitors next week.

2 Lunch [will be, will to be] ready in five minutes.

3 [Will it be, Will it is] cold tonight?

4 Dr. Patterson [will not be, will not to be] here tomorrow.

5 I think Serena Williams [will win, will winning] the tennis game.

6 The party [will start, will starts] at about 8:30.

7 If the weather is nice, [I will ride, I'm will ride] my bike to work.

8 The next train [will come, will coming] in six minutes.

9 When [will Helena have, Helena will has] her baby?

10 I called the refrigerator repairman. [He'll be, He's will be] here in an hour.

11 I promise [I won't be, I'll not be] late.

Practice 2

Rewrite the sentence with *will*.

Example:

1 It's going to be cold tonight.
It <u>will be cold</u> tonight.

2 Al isn't going to come to our party.
Al _____ .

3 She is going to be out of town next week.
She _____ next week.

4 Is your brother going to be a doctor?
_____ ?

5 The price of gas is going to go up.
_____ .

6 Our taxes are not going to come down.
Our taxes _____ .

7 When is he going to start his new job?
_____ ?

8 Who is going to help me?

_____ ?

9 I am not going to have an accident.

I _____ an accident.

10 You are going to enjoy your trip to Cancún.

You _____ to Cancún.

11 We are going to see you there.

We _____ .

FUTURE TIME EXPRESSIONS

Presentation

Future Time Expressions

Future time expressions tell when an event will happen. Many expressions begin with *this*, *next*, or *in*.

Rules	Examples
Use *this* with a specific time that is happening now or will start soon.	Ruth is arriving **this minute**.
	We'll finish the project **this week**.
Use *next* with a specific time period. The time period has not started yet.	The package will arrive **next week**.
	We are going on vacation **next Monday**.
Use *in* with an amount of time. The event will happen after that time passes.	I'll call you **in an hour**.
	My birthday is **in two weeks**.

Practice 1

Circle the letter of the correct word to complete each sentence.

Example:

1 *We will have visitors _____ week.*

  a *in*
  b *next*

2 Nora is going to get married _____ two months.

   a in

   b next

3 Kei is living with his parents now, but _____ year he's going to live with roommates.

   a in

   b next

4 Teacher: Your essays are due on Wednesday.

   Student: Do you mean tomorrow?

   Teacher: No, not tomorrow. _____ Wednesday.

   a in

   b Next

5 The television show started ten minutes ago. It will end _____ 45 minutes.

   a in

   b this

6 Parvin is going to visit her relatives in Iran _____ year.

   a in

   b next

7 It's going to rain _____ afternoon.

   a in

   b this

8 This class is going to end _____ ten minutes.

   a in

   b this

9 A: Are you flying to Philadelphia tomorrow?

   B: No. My schedule changed. I'm going to go _____ week.

   a this

   b in

10 A: When is your dental appointment?

   B: _____ Friday.

   a This

   b In

11 I'm busy now. I'll call you _____ a while.

   a in

   b this

Practice 2

Fill in the blank with *this*, *next*, or *in*.

Example:

1 *I'm working today, and I'm going to have dinner with my brother* <u>this</u> *evening.*

2 Yesterday was Jane's birthday. She was 12 years old. She will be 13 _____ year.

3 I'm tired. I don't want to go to work _____ morning.

4 Please be patient. I will answer your question _____ a minute.

5 A: When will the package arrive?
B: _____ two or three days.

6 A: When is your vacation?
B: _____ week. We're going to leave on Sunday and return on Friday.

7 A: It's 9:30 already. Where's the boss?
B: He won't be here _____ morning. He has an appointment at the bank.

8 Americans elect a new president every four years. There was an election last year. There will be another election _____ three years.

9 A: Are you busy at work right now?
B: Yes. We're always busy in November. But _____ month will be slow because of the holidays.

10 A: When can I talk to you about my test?
B: Come to my office _____ an hour.

11 A: Would you like to come over for dinner on Saturday?
B: Do you mean the day after tomorrow?
A: Yes.
B: Sorry, we already have plans _____ weekend.

Imperatives

Imperatives

Imperatives are sentences that give commands, advice, directions, or instructions. In an imperative sentence, the subject is always *you*, but we don't say it. Imperative sentences begin with the base form of verbs. You can use "please" to make imperatives more polite.

Forms	Examples
Affirmative	**Please sit** down.
	Take the plates and **put** them on the table.
Negative	**Don't (Do not) forget** to turn off the light.
	Please don't (do not) sing so loudly.

Practice 1

Read the paragraph. Circle 13 imperatives.

To cook perfect spaghetti or other pasta, follow these steps. First, fill a large pot full of cold water and let it boil. Don't cover the pot with a lid.

When the water boils, add one or two tablespoons of salt. The salt will make the pasta taste better. Don't add oil.

Cook the pasta for 8–12 minutes. Don't overcook it. When it's ready, it will be soft but a little chewy. (The Italians call this "al dente.")

Next, remove the pot from the heat and add a cup of cold water. This will stop the cooking.

Now drain the pasta in the sink. Then transfer it to a bowl. Finally, add your favorite sauce.

Practice 2

Fill in the blank with the affirmative or negative imperative form of the verb in parentheses.

Examples:

(wash) Please <u>wash</u> the dishes.

(not leave) <u>Don't leave</u> them in the sink.

Follow these tips to stay safe in an earthquake:

If you are indoors,

1 (move) _____ to a safe place.

2 (get) If possible, _____ under a desk or table.

3 (stay) _____ away from windows and bookcases.

4 (no use) _____ elevators.

5 (no go) _____ outside until the shaking stops.

If you are in bed,

6 (put) _____ a pillow over your head to protect it.

If you are outdoors,

7 (no stand) _____ near buildings or trees.

If you are driving,

8 (pull) _____ over to the side of the road.

Prepositions

PREPOSITIONS OF TIME

Presentation

Prepositions of Time

Prepositions of time answer the question *when?* The most common prepositions of time include *in, on, at,* and *from … to.* Prepositional phrases of time consist of a preposition of time + a noun; for example, *at night, in the spring.*

	Rules	Examples
Use *in* with	parts of the day*	in the morning, in the evening
	months	in December
	years	in 1975
	seasons	in the summer
Use *on* with	days of the week	on Tuesday
	specific dates	on November 13th
	holidays	on Thanksgiving
	special days	on my birthday
Use *at* with	specific times	at 3 o'clock, at 6 p.m., at noon, at midnight
Use *from … to* with	a span of time (the starting and ending points of a period of time)	from 2 to 4 a.m., from Monday to Friday, from January to June

*Exception: *at night*

Practice 1

Underline the correct preposition of time to complete the sentence.

Example:

1 *I can meet you [at, in, on] 3:30.*

2 A: Where are you going for the holidays?
B: [At, In, On] Christmas day we're going to be with my parents.

3 Aisha gets up [at, in, on] 5:00 a.m. and goes jogging.

4 Gina lived in Italy [for, from, in] 2005 [at, in, to] 2008.

5 We always go out to dinner [at, in, on] Sunday nights.

6 [At, In, On] winter there are only six hours of daylight.

7 Henry was born [at, in, on] 1988.

8 The school year will start [at, in, on] September 12.

9 We'll be in New York [for, from, on] three weeks.

10 William worked more than 200 hours [at, in, on] April.

Practice 2

Complete the sentence with the correct preposition of time.

America's space shuttle program operated <u>for</u> 30 years, _____ 1981 _____ 2011. The shuttles flew into space and back. They carried astronauts and equipment.

The first space shuttle, *Columbia*, went into space _____ April 12, 1981. It completed 28 trips. It was in space _____ a total of 300 days.

The last shuttle, *Atlantis*, completed its last flight _____ July 8, 2011.

Some of the "retired" shuttles are going to be in museums. For example, *Atlantis* will be at the Kennedy Space Center in Florida. The exhibit opened to the public _____ July 2013.

The shuttle *Endeavor* flew 25 missions _____ 1981 _____ 2011. Now visitors can see it at the California Science Center in Los Angeles. The exhibit opened _____ Tuesday, October 30, 2012.

PREPOSITIONS OF PLACE

Presentation

Prepositions of Place

Prepositions of place tell us *where* something is. Prepositional phrases of place consist of a preposition of place + a noun; for example, *at the market, on Main Street, next to the door.*

The most common prepositions of place are *in, on,* and *at.*

Below is a list of other prepositional phrases. The illustration of a bedroom will help you understand the meaning of these prepositional phrases.

Rules		Examples
Use *in* with	countries, states, and cities	in Malaysia, in New Jersey, in Portland
	the meaning of *inside* or in a defined space (e.g., rooms in a house, a park)	in the library, in the bedroom
Use *on* with	names of streets, roads, boulevards, etc.	on Sunset Boulevard
	the floor of a building	on the second floor
	the meaning of "on top of"	on the table
Use *at* with	addresses	at 1823 Spruce St.
	specific known places and buildings	at the airport, at the park, at the beach, at the Avon Theater

Practice 1

Circle the letter of the correct preposition.

Example:

1 *The bookstore is _____ Olive Street.*

  a on

  b *at*

  c *in*

2 Marrakesh is a city _____ Morocco.

  a on

  b at

  c in

3 The children are playing _____ the yard.

  a on

  b at

  c in

4 The White House is _____ 1600 Pennsylvania Avenue, Washington D.C.

  a on

  b at

  c in

5 The University Art Museum is located _____ Dodd Hall.

  a on

  b at

  c in

6 Child: Where's Daddy?

Mother: He's _____ his desk in the living room.

  a on

  b at

  c in

7 I live _____ Maple Street.

  a on

  b at

  c in

8 At night, the dog sleeps _____ the laundry room.

  a on

  b at

  c in

9 Tonight the Master Chorale will perform _____ Disney Concert Hall.

  a on

  b at

  c in

10 There's a small lake _____ the middle of the park.

  a on

  b at

  c in

Practice 2

Choose a preposition to complete the sentence about Ravi's room. Use each preposition only once.

next to	on top of	across from
above	in	between
near	in the middle of	

There are lamps _____ the file cabinets.

There are two file cabinets _____ the room.

The sofa is _____ the desk.

The bookshelf is _____ the plant.

There are windows _____ the sofa.

There is a rug _____ the room.

The sofa is _____ two file cabinets.

The plant is _____ the desk.

Present

SIMPLE PRESENT BE

Presentation

Simple Present *Be*

The simple present of *be* has three forms: *am*, *is*, and *are*. To form the negative, put *not* after the verb. To form questions, put the subject after the form of *be*.

Forms	Examples
Affirmative statements	I **am** a student.
	You **are** a good writer.
	He / She / It / Nancy **is** interesting.
	We **are** in New York.
	They / Nancy and Bill **are** Irish.
Negative statements	I **am not** ready.
	You **are not** my teacher.
	He / She / It / Luke **is not** Italian.
	We **are not** singers.
	They / The boys / Tom and Bill **are not** tired.
Subject pronouns with *be* can be made into contractions	**I'm** a student.
	You're a good writer.
	He's / **She's** / **It's** Italian.
	We're singers.
	They're happy.
Subject forms of *be* except *am* can be contracted in the negative.	**You're not** / **You aren't** silly.
	He's not / **He isn't** here.
	We're not / **We aren't** going yet.
	They're not / **They aren't** Russian.
	You are not (aren't) ready.
Questions	**Am I** pretty?
	Are you ready?
	What **is he** doing?

Practice 1

Complete each sentence with the correct affirmative form of _be_.

Example:

1 Sunday <u>is</u> the first day of the week.
2 You _____ in my French class.
3 Linda _____ my partner for this exercise.
4 Javier and I _____ from the same city.
5 He _____ in the cafeteria.
6 I _____ very tired today.
7 You and Tina _____ good writers.
8 It _____ Friday.
9 He _____ an excellent tennis player.
10 They _____ serious students.

Practice 2

Complete each sentence with the correct negative form of _be_.

Example:

1 Today <u>is not</u> my birthday.

2 It _____ cold today.

3 They _____ in my math class.

4 You _____ in our group.

5 Martina and I _____ sisters.

6 She _____ a lawyer.

7 Professor Snow and Professor Brinton _____ in their offices.

8 I _____ ready for this test.

9 Andrew and I _____ from Peru.

10 You and Barbara _____ good swimmers.

THE SIMPLE PRESENT

Copyright © 2017 by Pearson Education, Inc. Duplication is not permitted.

Presentation

The Simple Present

- The simple present uses the base form of the verb for all subjects except third-person singular (*he*, *she*, and *it*).
- For third-person singular, add *–s* to the base form of the verb. Add *–es* if the verb ends in *–ss*, *–sh*, *–zz*, *–ch*, or *–x*.
- *Have* is irregular in the third-person singular affirmative—*has*.
- To make verbs negative, use *do not / don't* or *does not / doesn't* + base form.

Use the simple present to talk about:

- Facts

  Many birds **fly** south for the winter.

  Penguins **don't fly**.

- Habits or regular routines

  I always **wash** my hands before I **eat**.

  Lana **doesn't eat** meat.

- Opinions

  Enya **doesn't like** candy.

  She **prefers** fruit.

- Ownership

  We **have** an old car.

  Fred **doesn't own** a car.

Forms	Affirmative	Negative
Regular verbs	I / You / We / They **dance**.	I / You / We / They **do not / don't dance**.
	He / She / It **dances**.	He / She / It **does not / doesn't dance**.
Have	I / You / We / They **have** a problem.	I / You / We / They **do not / don't have** time.
	He / She / It **has** a problem.	He / She / It **does not / doesn't have** time.

Practice 1

Complete the sentence with the simple present affirmative form of the verb in parentheses.

Example:

1 *My friends and I <u>like</u> (like) to eat lunch together.*
2 I _____ (have) a photo of my family in my wallet.
3 Some people _____ (believe) the earth is flat.
4 Nathan _____ (call) his parents twice a week.
5 That restaurant _____ (have) slow service.
6 Babies _____ (sleep) a lot.
7 Edna _____ (speak) French very well.
8 My friend and I _____ (study) together every day.
9 She _____ (wash) her car every week.
10 The soup _____ (taste) delicious.
11 Those plants _____ (need) a lot of water.

Practice 2

Complete the sentence with the simple present negative form of the verb in parentheses.

Example:

1 *Mrs. Adams is 89 years old. She <u>doesn't walk</u> (walk) well.*
2 The child _____ (like) to be alone.
3 I _____ (feel) well today.
4 It _____ (snow) in Death Valley.
5 Thomas _____ (have) time to go shopping today.
6 Clara _____ (understand) the directions.
7 We _____ (want) more homework.
8 That store _____ (sell) computers.
9 In the United States, most people _____ (speak) Tagalog.
10 You _____ (need) to come early.
11 They _____ (know) the answer to the question.

FREQUENCY ADVERBS

Presentation

Frequency Adverbs

Frequency adverbs answer the question "how often?" For example, I *always eat lunch at 12:30 P.M.* Common frequency adverbs are: *always, usually, often, sometimes, rarely, seldom,* and *never.*

Position of Frequency Adverbs:

- Adverbs of frequency normally come before the main verb.
- Adverbs of frequency normally come after *be* and *not.*
- *Usually* and *sometimes* can also come at the beginning of the sentence.
- In negative sentences, put *always, usually,* and *often* after *not.*
- In negative sentences, *sometimes* should go at the beginning of the sentence.

Meanings of Frequency Adverbs:

Adverbs	Examples
always (100%)	The baby **always** sleeps in the afternoon.
usually (80–90%)	The gardener **usually** arrives around 11 a.m.
often (70–80%)	Mina **often** takes the train to work.
sometimes (50%)	**Sometimes** we play cards on Friday night.
rarely, seldom (20–30%)	I **rarely** eat dessert.
never (0%)	Candace is **never** late.

Practice 1

Read the sets of sentences. Underline the sentence that is incorrect.

1 She is seldom late.
Never she is late.
Occasionally she is late.

2 Sometimes Cathy eats dessert.
Cathy always eats dessert.
Cathy eats dessert never.

3 The train is often late.
Rarely the train is late.
The train is sometimes late.

4 Raul takes sometimes the bus to work.
Raul often takes the bus to work.
Raul rarely takes the bus to work.

5 Kei doesn't have usually an 8:00 a.m. class.
Usually Kei doesn't have an 8:00 a.m. class.
Kei doesn't usually have an 8:00 a.m. class.

6 Mr. Holt usually eats breakfast at home.
Mr. Holt often eats breakfast at home.
Mr. Holt eats breakfast at home rarely.

7 Ray never sends text messages during class.
Sometimes Ray sends text messages during class.
Ray sends text messages often during class.

8 Bus drivers in my town are often rude.
Bus drivers in my town never are rude.
Bus drivers in my town are sometimes rude.

9 It doesn't usually rain in March.
Often it doesn't rain in March.
It seldom rains in March.

10 Bella rarely makes spelling mistakes.
Often Bella makes spelling mistakes.
Bella sometimes makes spelling mistakes.

11 Gina is sometimes late to work.
Gina never is late to work.
Gina is often late to work.

Practice 2

Rewrite the sentence, adding the adverb of frequency in parentheses. You can write some sentences in more than one way.

Example:

1 *(never) Georgia is late to work.*
   Georgia is never late to work.

2 (always) My family eats dinner together.

_____

3 (usually) Linda finishes work at 5:30.

_____

4 (often) My friends and I don't study together.

_____

5 (sometimes) Marwan does not understand his teacher.

_____

6 (seldom) The mail is late.

_____

7 (never) The restaurant is open on Christmas.

_____

8 (usually) My kids have activities after school.

_____

9 (often) Mr. and Mrs. Short go out for breakfast.

_____

10 (never) Susan's dog barks.

_____

11 (always) Exercise is not healthy.

_____

PRESENT PROGRESSIVE

Present Progressive

We use the present progressive to talk about things that are happening now or in the future. For example, we use it to describe what people are doing or what they are wearing now. We also use it to discuss what they will be doing in the future.

Examples:

I am wearing a tie. (present)

We are leaving for Aruba tomorrow. (future)

Forms

The form of the present progressive is *be (not)* + verb + *–ing*.

Spelling

Forms	Singular	Plural
Affirmative statements	I **am eating**.	We / They **are eating**.
	You **are eating**.	
	He / She / It **is eating**.	
Negative statements	I **am not working**.	We / They **are not working**.
	You **are not working**.	
	He / She / It **is not working**.	
Yes/No questions	**Am** I **doing** it correctly?	**Are** we / they **going**?
	Are you **going**?	
	Is he / she / it **working**?	
Wh- questions	What **am** I **doing** wrong?	When **are** we / they **going**?
	Where **are** you **going**?	
	How **is** he / she / it **working**?	

Rules	Examples
Add *-ing* to most verbs.	play > playing
	sing > singing
	work > working
If a verb ends in e, drop the e and add *-ing*.	make > making

If a verb ends in consonant-vowel-consonant, then double the last consonant and add -ing.	sit > sitting
Do not double w or x.	throw > throwing
Do not double the final consonant when the last syllable is unstressed.	begin > beginning happen > happening

Practice 1

Complete each sentence with the affirmative present progressive form of the verb in parentheses.

Example:

1 It is <u>raining</u> (rain).

2 My two brothers _____ (play) basketball outside.

3 My younger brother _____ (win).

4 Some neighbors _____ (watch).

5 Inside the house, my mother _____ (talk) loudly on the phone.

6 I _____ (study) for a test.

7 All the noise _____ (bother) me.

8 He _____ (have) a good time.

9 A: _____ (go, you) to the football game tonight?

    B: Yes, I am.

10 A: _____ (come, your sister), too?

    B: Yes, she is.

11 A: What time _____ (leave, you) your house?

    B: Around 6:30. Do you need a ride?

Practice 2

Complete each sentence with the negative present progressive form of the verb in parentheses.

Example:

1 The sun <u>is not shining</u> (shine).

2 A: How's the weather?

    B: It's calm today. It _____ (rain).

3 The wind _____ (blow).

4 It is warm, so most people _____ (wear) jackets or coats.

5 A: Hello, can I please speak to Marianne?

B: Sorry, she _____ (work) today.

6 A: What's for dinner? I love your lasagna.

B: Sorry, I _____ (make) lasagna this time.

7 You _____ (listen) to me. Please pay attention!

8 My roommate and I enjoy jogging, but we _____ (jog) today. We don't have time.

9 You _____ (smile). What's wrong?

10 There was a big storm last night, so the buses _____ (run) today.

11 The flowers I planted _____ (grow) well. Maybe they need more water.

SIMPLE PRESENT VS. PRESENT PROGRESSIVE

Presentation

Simple Present vs. Present Progressive

The simple present and present progressive have different meanings, and we use them with different time expressions.

Rules	Examples
Use the present progressive for actions that are happening now.	The teacher **is correcting** papers.
	She **isn't planning** lessons.
Use the present progressive for actions that are happening for a period of time that includes this moment.	Jun **is studying** in Texas these days.
	We **are living** in Miami for now.
The present progressive can refer to the future. These time expressions are commonly used with it: *right now, at this moment, today, these days, this morning / afternoon / evening, this week / month / year.*	It **is snowing** today.
	I'm working at home this week.

Use the present progressive with *have* when it means eating, drinking, or experiencing something (such as a test or a party).	We**'re having** a party at our apartment on Friday night.
	We**'re having** salad for dinner.

Rules	Examples
Use the simple present to talk about habits, routines, or facts that are not expected to change.	Alberto **swims** every day.
	Saudi Arabia **exports** oil.
Use the simple present with frequency adverbs.	It **never rains** on my birthday.
	Sometimes Eva **wakes up** early.
Use the simple present, not the present progressive, with such non-action verbs as *have, be, look, want, believe, know, need, hear, see, like, love,* and *think*.	I **want** a cup of coffee.
	We **own** a house in San Diego.
	I **think** you're nice.
	She **looks** happy.
Some non-action verbs can take the present progressive, but the meaning is different. Some of these verbs include *have* (= "eat" or "drink"), *think* (= "using my mind"), *love* (= "enjoy"), and *see* (= "date").	I **have** two cats. *(non-action)* I**'m having** dinner right now. *(action)*
	I **think** you're wonderful. *(non-action)* I**'m thinking** about my brother. *(action)*
	I **love** my sister. *(non-action)* I**'m loving** this weather. *(action)*
	I **see** Dana. *(non-action)* I**'m seeing** Dana. *(action)*

Practice 1

Read the sentences. Underline *Correct* or *Incorrect*.

Example:

1 *I am wanting a new car.*
Correct
Incorrect

2 A: How's the weather today?
B: It rains.

Correct
Incorrect

3 Close the window. The neighbors are fighting again.

Correct
Incorrect

4 Karen is having a very big family.

Correct
Incorrect

5 Mr. Grey is taking the bus downtown every day.

Correct
Incorrect

6 Steve shops at the supermarket right now.

Correct
Incorrect

7 We are having fish for dinner.

Correct
Incorrect

8 We are needing to take a break.

Correct
Incorrect

9 I'm believing in you.

Correct
Incorrect

10 The students are not paying attention.

Correct
Incorrect

11 Bonnie is always finishing her homework on time.

Correct
Incorrect

Practice 2

Underline the correct form of the verb to complete each sentence.

Example:

1 I _____ *any help right now, thanks.*
am not needing
<u>*don't need*</u>

2 Please don't go in the baby's room. She _____.
is sleeping
sleeps

3 Anna _____ a singing lesson once a week.
has
is having

4 A: What's that noise?
B: What noise? I _____ anything.
am not hearing
don't hear

5 The washing machine is leaking. I _____ a repair company now.
am calling
call

6 You _____ fantastic.

are looking

look

7 A: Hello, is Carla home?

B: No. She _____ the dog at the moment.

is walking

walks

8 My cousin and his wife _____ any children.

aren't having

don't have

9 Franco _____ a friend in New Orleans this week.

is visiting

visits

10 A: Look! There's a whale!

B: Where? I _____ anything.

am not seeing

don't see

11 Human hair _____ quickly.

grows

is growing

Pronouns

SUBJECT PRONOUNS

Subject Pronouns

Pronouns take the place of nouns. Subject pronouns can be the subject of a sentence. They can also take the place of proper nouns; that is, the names of people or places.

Examples:

Robert is my younger brother. He is taller than I am.

The Grand Canyon is beautiful. It is also large.

Use *it* to talk about time, the weather, the day, the season, and the date.

Examples:

It is Tuesday.

It's sunny.

Forms	Singular	Plural
1st person	I	we
2nd person	you	you
3rd person	he, she, it	they

Practice 1

Circle the letter of the correct pronoun to complete each sentence.

1 My neighbor is very kind. _____ often helps me.
   a They
   b She

2 Zena and Marco are very busy. _____ work and go to school.
   a They
   b He

3 The weather is good today. _____ is sunny and warm.
   a It
   b They

4 In that photo, Carlos is laughing. _____ looks happy.
   a It
   b He

Copyright © 2017 by Pearson Education, Inc. Duplication is not permitted.

5 My mother and I share clothes. _____ wear the same size.
  a We
  b They

6 Today is October 27. _____ is my birthday.
  a It
  b He

7 The plants are dry. _____ need water.
  a It
  b They

8 I like Saturday. _____ is my favorite day of the week.
  a She
  b It

9 The United States and Canada are in North America. _____ are neighbors.
  a They
  b It

10 Teddy and I love classical music. _____ like to attend concerts together.
  a We
  b They

Practice 2

Fill in the blank with the correct subject pronoun.

Example:

1 *Cinzia is in my English class. She is a good student.*

2 That man's name is Pietro. _____ is from Italy.

3 My name is Alida. _____ am from the Netherlands.

4 What time is it? _____ is 3 o'clock.

5 Please call me. _____ forgot your textbook in my car.

6 You and I are partners. _____ need to choose a time to meet.

7 Shakira is a popular female singer. _____ has more than 50 million friends on Facebook.

8 These brownies are fresh. _____ are delicious.

9 Today isn't November 5. _____ is November 6.

10 My brother and I look alike. _____ have red hair.

11 My paragraph has mistakes. _____ need to write it again.

OBJECT PRONOUNS

Presentation

Object Pronouns

Pronouns take the place of nouns. Object pronouns replace nouns that come after the verb (direct object) or after the direct object (indirect object). They can also come after prepositions (object of the preposition).

Pronouns	After a Verb	After a Preposition
me	Can you see **me**?	Do you want to come to the concert with **me**?
you	I can't hear **you**.	Can I go with **you** to the store?
him, her, it	Mr. Sanders is my boss. I respect **him** a lot.	I mailed the check to **her**.
us	Your explanation helped **us**.	Some tourists sat next to **us**.
them	Linda is far away from her family. She misses **them** very much.	My parents are traveling in Australia. I haven't heard from **them**.

Practice 1

Circle the letter of the correct pronoun to complete each sentence.

1 My roommate's name is Sarawong. He is from Thailand. I like _____ a lot.
  a him
  b he

2 You can have this shirt. I don't want _____ .
  a its
  b it

3 When you see Barbara, please give a message to _____ .
  a her
  b she

4 We should ask the teacher to help _____ .
  a we
  b us

5 Where are Ted and Alice? I don't see _____ .

   a they

   b them

6 Thank you for sending that link to _____ .

   a me

   b my

7 I bought apples for _____ .

   a you

   b your

8 The children are sitting on the floor. I'm going to walk around _____ .

   a they

   b them

9 Happy Birthday, Somsak! This gift is from _____ .

   a we

   b us

10 Beyonce is an interesting person. I like reading about _____ .

   a her

   b she

Practice 2

Complete the sentence. Replace the underlined word or words with an object pronoun.

Example:

1 *I love you. Do you love <u>me</u>?*

2 I can't lift this box. Can you help _____ ?

3 Shira took the bar exam to become a lawyer. She is not sure if she passed _____ .

4 Francois can't find his keys. Maybe he left _____ at his office.

5 I can't hear you. Can you hear _____ ?

6 I emailed Ahmed and invited _____ to dinner.

7 We went to a lecture about the city of Jerusalem. I would love to visit _____ .

8 I called Mary. I asked _____ to drive me to the doctor.

9 When my wife and I go out, my mother often babysits for _____ .

10 I don't like driving in heavy traffic. It makes _____ nervous.

11 We were happy when our classmate invited _____ to her wedding.

Past

VERB BE

Presentation

Simple Past: Verb *Be*

- Use the simple past for actions that began and ended in the past.
- The simple past of *be* has two forms: *was* and *were*.
- Use *was* for 1st and 3rd person singular subjects. Use *were* for 2nd person singular and all plural subjects.
- To form negatives of the simple past, put *not* after *was / were*. You can use contractions: *was not = wasn't, were not = weren't*.
- To form questions, put *was / were* before the subject and after the question word.

Forms	Examples
Statements	I / He / She / It **was** late.
	You / We / They **were** late.
Negatives	I / He / She / It **was not / wasn't** ready.
	You / We / They **were not /weren't** ready.
Questions	**Was** I / he / she / it correct?
	Were you / we / they on time?
	Why **was** I / he / she/ it wrong?
	When **were** you / we / they in France?

Practice 1

Underline the correct form to complete each sentence.

Example:

1 *Yesterday [was, were] November 5th.*

2 We [were, was] at a baseball game yesterday afternoon.

3 It [was, were] a cold day.

4 They [weren't, wasn't] home.

5 I [was, were] with my grandmother.

6 When [were, was] you in Italy?

7 [Was, Were] John late for work this morning?

8 She [was not, were not] happy with her test score.

9 Karen and I [were, was] friends for many years.

10 Thomas [was not, were not] in our class.

11 [Were, Was] the children tired?

Practice 2

Rewrite the sentence in the simple past.

Example:

1 *Where are you?*
Where were you?

2 Gabriel is absent.
Yesterday, Gabriel _____ .

3 I am not late.
This morning, I _____ .

4 Are you confused?
_____ ?

5 When are you in your office?
_____ ?

6 Manya and I are ready for the test.
Manya and I _____ .

7 Sima is not in our group.
Sima _____ .

8 Is your interview on Thursday?
_____ ?

9 What is the correct answer?
_____ ?

10 We are not home.
Yesterday evening we _____ .

11 Who is the captain of the team?
_____ ?

REGULAR VERBS

Presentation

Simple Past: Regular Verbs

We use the simple past for actions that began and ended in the past. Verbs in the simple past have regular and irregular forms.

Forms of Past Regular Verbs	
Rules	**Examples**
To form affirmative sentences, add -ed to verbs.	I **waited** for an hour.
	They **missed** the bus.
To form negative sentences, use *did not* + verb. *Did not* contracts to *didn't*.	She **did not / didn't say** anything.
	We **did not / didn't go**.
To form yes/no questions, use *did* + subject + verb. To form *wh-* questions, use *wh-* word + *did* + subject + verb.	**Did he finish?**
	When did you leave?

Spelling Rules	
Rules	*Examples*
Add -ed to most verbs.	listen > listened
When the base form ends in e, add -d.	dance > danced
When the base form ends in y, change the y to i and add -ed.	hurry > hurried
Double the final consonant and add -ed when the base form ends in consonant + vowel + consonant (CVC) or the last syllable is stressed.	plan > planned
	ship > shipped
	permit > permitted
Do not double final w, x, and y.	box > boxed
	play > played
	bow > bowed

Practice 1

Complete the sentence with the affirmative past tense form of the verb in parentheses.

Example:

1 I _waited_ (wait) more than an hour for the bus.

2 Mina _____ (ask) her roommate for help.

3 Hans _____ (decide) to fly home for Christmas.

4 Rina and Max _____ (study) together last night.

5 Carlos _____ (stop) drinking coffee to save money.

6 We _____ (stay) at the party until 2 A.M.

7 A plumber _____ (fix) our leaky sink.

8 Zachary _____ (hurry) to catch the elevator.

9 The mail _____ (arrive) at 4 P.M. yesterday.

10 Anna _____ (prefer) to speak English with her friends.

11 My aunt _____ (visit) me last week.

Practice 2

Complete the sentence. Use the same verb, but make it negative.

Example:

1 *I often walk to work, but yesterday I* did not walk .

2 Donna usually cooks dinner for her family, but last night she _____ .

3 I usually play soccer on Wednesdays, but yesterday I _____ .

4 It usually rains in April, but last April it _____ .

5 Jun talks to his father almost every day, but yesterday he and his father _____ .

6 Normally it snows in December, but last December it _____ .

7 We usually go out to breakfast on Sunday, but last Sunday we _____ out.

8 Lidia usually waits for her friends after class, but this afternoon she _____ .

9 Patricia often watches television in the evening, but yesterday evening she _____ television.

10 Olivia usually walks her dog before work, but this morning she _____ the dog.

11 Paolo usually washes his car on weekends, but last weekend he _____ it.

12 The gardener usually comes on Tuesday, but last Tuesday he _____ .

13 Flora writes in her journal almost every day, but yesterday she _____ anything.

IRREGULAR VERBS

Simple Past: Irregular Verbs

We use the simple past for actions that began and ended in the past. The simple past has both regular and irregular forms. All regular verbs end in *-ed*. Irregular verbs have special forms. You need to study and memorize them.

Base Form	Simple Past
be	was, were
become	became
begin	began
break	broke
bring	brought
build	built
come	came
drive	drove
fall	fell
feel	felt
find	found
fly	flew
get	got
give	gave
go	went
grow	grew
have	had
hit	hit
know	knew
leave	left
make	made
say	said
see	saw
sell	sold
sleep	slept
speak	spoke
spend	spent
take	took
teach	taught
tell	told
think	thought
wake up	woke up

Practice 1

Underline 11 irregular simple past verbs in the paragraphs.

Last night I studied until 10. Then I walked my dog.

I usually speak to my grandmother once a day. Yesterday evening I called her and we talked for about ten minutes. I told her I planned to come visit her in the morning. Then we said good night.

This morning I called my grandmother at about 9 a.m. To my surprise, she did not answer the phone. I waited half an hour, and then I tried again. Again there was no answer. I began to worry. What if she had an accident? I decided to go see her.

I got in my car and drove to her apartment. When I arrived, I knocked on her door and called her name. I was nervous. But 30 seconds later she opened the door.

"Grandma, are you OK?" I asked her.

"Yes, why?" she answered.

"Well, I called you three times this morning, and you didn't answer. What happened?"

"Nothing happened, dear. I stayed up half the night reading a book, so this morning I slept late. I just woke up. Would you like to come in and eat breakfast with me?"

Practice 2

Complete the sentence with the past form of the irregular verb in parentheses.

Example:

1 *Mrs. Barnston sold (sell) her car.*

2 Jordan _____ (become) an independent country in 1946.

3 My phone, my hair dryer, and my microwave oven all _____ (break) in the same week.

4 Sandra _____ (feel) tired after running 3 miles.

5 I didn't feel well, so I _____ (leave) my French class early.

6 Sammy _____ (make) three mistakes on his geometry test.

7 Last year, Jehan _____ (see) snow for the first time.

8 Barbara _____ (spend) last summer in Cameroon.

9 Who _____ (take) my coffee cup?

10 My father _____ (teach) me how to drive a car.

11 I _____ (think) about the problem for a long time.

TIME EXPRESSIONS

Simple Past: Time Expressions

Past time expressions tell when something happened. They can come at the beginning or at the end of a sentence. If a time expression with a preposition or adverb begins a sentence, a comma often follows it.

Time Expressions	Examples
yesterday	**Yesterday** was my daughter's birthday.
last + a period of time (last week, last month, last year)	**Last week** Roberto worked 60 hours.
an amount of time + *ago*	I visited Australia **five years ago**.
in + a month, season, or year	Susan got married **in 1999**.
on + a day or date	**On July 6, 2010**, the Ghosh family arrived in the United States.
for + an amount of time	Krista waited **for 45 minutes**.

Practice 1

Read the sentence with a past time expression. Underline *Correct* or *Incorrect*.

Example:

1 *Natalie went to the doctor in Tuesday.*
Correct

Incorrect

2 Our final English exam was ago last Friday.
Correct

Incorrect

3 My grandparents were married on 60 years.
Correct

Incorrect

4 Malina didn't go to work yesterday.

Correct

Incorrect

5 Enrico and Nina yesterday left to go on their honeymoon.

Correct

Incorrect

6 Pamela started her job in March 2.

Correct

Incorrect

7 Marco studied in Japan on last semester.

Correct

Incorrect

8 Paul went on 12 business trips last year.

Correct

Incorrect

9 We watched TV for three hours.

Correct

Incorrect

10 My wedding was on the spring.

Correct

Incorrect

11 My parents were in Europe for a month.

Correct

Incorrect

Practice 2

Underline the correct time expression to complete the sentence.

Example:

1 *I spent a summer in London* [three years ago, for three years].

2 [Last, In] month, Brad went on a business trip.

3 He was in Toronto [for, on] a week.

4 He was also there [two years ago, in two years].

5 The Smiths remodeled their house [in, on] 2008.

6 Construction started [on, in] May 1.

7 The Smiths lived in a hotel [for, on] about three months.

8 They moved back into their house [in, on] October.

9 [On, In] August 23, 2011, a hurricane damaged the Smiths' house.

10 They started a new construction project two months [ago, on].

11 They got a new roof [last week, week ago].

There is and There are

THERE IS / THERE ARE

Presentation

There is / There are

- *There is* and *there are* are expressions that tell us how many or much there is or are of something, or whether something exists.
- Use *there is* for singular nouns and for noncount nouns.
- Use *there are* for plural count nouns.
- *There is / there are* is not the subject of a sentence. The noun that follows it is the subject.

Examples:

Singular: There is a white <u>cat</u> in the yard.

Plural: There are <u>birds</u> in the trees.

Noncount: There is <u>mail</u> for you.

Rules	Examples
The verb *be* agrees with the subject.	There **is a chance** of rain.
	There **are three apples** in the basket.
Do not confuse *there are* with *they are.* Use *there are* to introduce a topic. Use *they are* instead of repeating a noun.	**There are** two apple trees in my garden.
	They ~~The two apple trees~~ **are** more than fifty years old.
Do not confuse *there* with *their.* Use *there* + *is / are.* Use *their* + noun to show possession.	**There is** a white cat in my yard. It does not belong to my neighbors. **Their** cat is black.
There is can be contracted to *there's. There's* is usually used in spoken English. *There are* cannot be contracted. *They're* means "they are."	**There's** time to see your friends.
	There are two people outside. **They're** waiting for you.

Practice 1

Complete the sentence with *there is* or *there are*.

Example:

1 _There are_ several trees in my back yard.

2 _____ a fireplace in my living room.

3 _____ paintings on the wall.

4 _____ large windows.

5 _____ a lot of light all day.

6 _____ comfortable furniture.

7 _____ a piano.

8 _____ a coffee table.

9 _____ magazines on the coffee table.

10 _____ fruit on the coffee table.

11 _____ shoes on the floor.

Practice 2

Underline the correct answer to complete each sentence.

Example:

1 *[There are, They are] two towns called Oceanside in the United States.*

[They are, There are] in different states.

2 [There are, Their] two students from Chile in my English class.

[Their, They are] names are Irma and Andres.

[They are, There are] from the same town.

3 [There are, They are] three girls in Sarah's family.

[They are, There are] close in age.

[Their, They are] personalities are very different.

4 [There are, Their] lots of magazines in my dentist's office.

[They are, There are] not new.

5 [There are, They are] two dogs next door.

[Their, They are] owners are not home very much.

SUBJECT-VERB AGREEMENTS WITH THERE IS / THERE ARE

Presentation

Subject-Verb Agreement with *There is / There are*

In sentences with *there is / there are*, the subject comes after the verb *is / are*. The verb must agree with the subject that follows it.

Examples:

Singular subject: **There is a family** of squirrels in the tree.

Plural subject: **There are two apples** in the bowl.

To make *there is* or *there are* negative, add *no* after *is* or *are*. Study the affirmative and negative forms of *there is / there are* in the chart.

Negative Forms	Examples
There is no + singular noun or noncount noun	**There is / There's no elevator** in the building.
	There is / There's no time to waste.
There are no + plural noun	**There are no trains** after midnight.

Practice 1

Underline *is* or *are* to complete each sentence.

Example:

1 There _____ two cars in the driveway.

is

<u>are</u>

2 There _____ a Southwest Airlines flight to San Francisco at 7 o'clock this evening.

is

are

3 Unfortunately, there _____ no seats in economy class.

is

are

4 There _____ a waiting list for seats.

is

are

5 There _____ already six names on it.

is

are

6 There _____ no chance I will get on the flight.

is

are

7 Maybe there _____ a later flight on another airline.

is

are

8 It's only 2 P.M. There _____ time to make a reservation.

is

are

9 I will get to San Francisco by midnight if there _____ no problems.

is

are

Practice 2

**Look at the picture of a bedroom. Complete each sentence with *There is*,
There is no, *There are*, or *There are no*.**

Example:

1 <u>There is</u> *a dresser in the bedroom.*

2 _____ a bed in the bedroom.

3 _____ picture frames on the dresser.

4 _____ two night stands.

5 _____ TV in the bedroom.

6 _____ a vase on the desk.

7 _____ flowers in the vase.

8 _____ fireplace in the bedroom.

9 _____ a lot of light.

10 _____ art on the wall.

11 _____ people in the room.

SENTENCE STRUCTURE

Coordinating Conjunctions

COORDINATING CONJUNCTION AND

Presentation

Use *and* to add information.

Rules	Examples
Use *and* to connect two subjects, two verbs, or two objects in a simple sentence. Do not use a comma before or after *and*. Use a plural verb when you connect subjects.	Coffee **and** tea are popular hot drinks in North America. *(two subjects)*
	James ate dinner **and** washed the dishes. *(two verbs)*
	Janice can speak Spanish **and** German. *(two objects)*
Use *and* to connect two adjectives or two adverbs.	Herman is tall **and** thin. She speaks slowly **and** clearly.
Use *and* to connect two independent clauses. Use a comma before *and*.	Our hotel room was beautiful, **and** the food was excellent.

Practice 1

Combine the sentences into one sentence with *and*. Do not use a comma. Change the verb to plural if necessary.

Example:

1 *Jenna is from Boston. Larry is from Boston.*
   Jenny and Larry are from Boston.

2 Oranges have vitamin C. Strawberries have vitamin C.
   _____ vitamin C.

3 Jason runs every day. Jason lifts weights every day.
   Jason _____ every day.

4 Kathy bought a bag of potatoes. Kathy bought a loaf of bread.

Kathy _____ bread.

5 The lemonade is cold. The lemonade is sweet.

The lemonade _____ .

6 Chile is in South America. Peru is in South America.

_____ South America.

7 She talks quickly. She talks loudly.

She _____ .

8 Horses can swim. Cows can swim.

_____ .

9 Susan likes pop music. Susan likes jazz.

Susan _____ .

10 Marta sells toys online. Her mother sells toys online.

_____ online.

11 Winters in Minnesota are cold. Winters in Minnesota are wet.

Winters _____ .

Practice 2

Combine the two sentences into one sentence with *and*. Use a comma. Change capital letters to lowercase letters as needed.

Example:

1 *I have a big dog. His name is Rocky.*

I have a big dog, and his name is *Rocky.*

2 The baby was tired. She began to cry.

The baby _____ to cry.

3 Tom is cooking dinner. Jane is watching the news.

Tom _____ the news.

4 Ben works in the daytime. He goes to school at night.

Ben works _____ at night.

5 It rained on Monday. It snowed on Tuesday.

It rained _____ on Tuesday.

6 Sima walks to school. Don rides his bike.

Sima _____ his bike.

7 Steven has an iPod. He takes it everywhere.

Steven _____ everywhere.

8 There was a fire. Many houses burned.

There _____ burned.

9 I bought a flute. I'm learning how to play it.

I bought _____ to play it.

10 I forgot to water the plant. It died.

I _____ died.

11 It's late. It's time to go home.

It's _____ go home.

COORDINATING CONJUNCTION BUT

Presentation

Use *but* to join two different or opposite ideas. You can also use it when the second idea is surprising.

Rules	Examples
Use *but* to connect two adjectives or two adverbs. Do not use a comma before or after *but*.	Janos is poor **but** happy.
	I speak French a lot **but** badly.
Use *but* to connect two simple sentences. Use a comma before *but*.	Junko didn't study, **but** she got a good grade.

Practice 1

Combine the sentences into one sentence with *but*. Do not use a comma.

Example:

1 *Sandy is small. Sandy is strong.*

  <u>Sandy is small but strong</u> .

2 She talks quickly. She talks clearly.

  _____ .

3 The day was cold. The day was clear.

_____ .

4 My dogs are big. My dogs are gentle.

_____ .

5 The test was long. The test was easy.

_____ .

6 The food was simple. The food was tasty.

_____ .

7 Our teacher is strict. Our teacher is fair.

_____ .

8 Thomas is smart. Thomas is disorganized.

_____ .

9 Mark drives quickly. Mark drives carefully.

_____ .

10 The course was difficult. The course was useful.

_____ .

11 Roller coasters are scary. Roller coasters are exciting.

_____ .

Practice 2

Combine the two simple sentences into one sentence with _but_. Use a comma. Change capital letters to lowercase letters as needed.

Example:

1 _Charles like cats. He doesn't like dogs._

Charles _likes cats, but he doesn't like_ _dogs._

2 I want to go with you. I have to study.

I want _____ to study.

3 David works in the city. He doesn't live there.

David works _____ there.

4 The furniture is expensive. It is not comfortable.

The furniture _____ comfortable.

5 The flowers are pretty. They smell bad.

The flowers _____ bad.

6 The music was great. It was too loud.

The music _____ loud.

7 The work is hard. It is interesting.

_____ interesting.

8 Sharon loves to eat. She hates to cook.

Sharon _____ cook.

9 The shoes were ugly. They were comfortable.

The shoes _____ comfortable.

10 I sent Tomiko a message. She didn't reply.

I sent _____ reply.

11 Peter only slept three hours. He isn't tired.

Peter only _____ tired.

COORDINATING CONJUNCTION OR

Presentation

Use *or* for a possibility or choice.

Rules	Examples
Use *or* to connect two words or phrases. Do not use a comma before or after *or*.	Sarah **or** Franco will wash the car. *(two subjects)*
	Hong will read a book **or** watch TV. *(two verbs)*
	Do you want meat **or** fish? *(two objects)*
Use *or* to connect two simple sentences. Use a comma before *or*.	I can drive to work**, or** I can ride my bike.

Practice 1

Combine the sentences into one sentence with *or*. Do not use a comma.

Example:

1 *Joyce likes Italian dressing. Joyce likes Thousand Island dressing.*

　Joyce like Italian or Thousand Island *dressing.*

2 Zach will bring a cake. Rina will bring a cake.

　_____

3 Steven swims every day. Steven runs 3 miles every day.

　_____ every day.

4 We're going to have pizza. We're going to have hamburgers.

　_____ .

5 Katrina will buy a sports car. Katrina will buy a motorcycle.

　Katrina _____ .

6 Dr. Haas can help you. Dr. Cheng can help you.

　_____ .

7 She eats scrambled eggs every morning. She eats cereal every morning.

　_____ every morning.

8 I like spaghetti with tomato sauce. I like spaghetti with pesto sauce.

　_____ sauce.

9 Susan reads the newspaper before work. Susan listens to the news before work.

　Susan _____ before work.

10 Marta will walk the dog. Her mother will walk the dog.

　_____ the dog.

11 Linda will phone her mother. Linda will email her mother

　_____ .

Practice 2

Combine the two sentences into one sentence with *or*. Use a comma.

Example:

1 *I will go home by bus. I will walk.*

　I will *go home by bus, or I will* *walk.*

2 Are you from Italy? Are you from France?

　Are you _____ France?

3 Jane will stay in school. She will get a job.

Jane will _____ a job.

4 Mehdi will do the project alone. He will find a partner.

Mehdi will _____ a partner.

5 I'll wear an old dress. I'll buy something new.

I'll wear _____ new.

6 We can carpool. We can meet at the restaurant.

We _____ at the restaurant.

7 They will look for a cheap hotel. They will camp out.

They will _____ camp out.

8 Maria is telling the truth. She is lying.

Maria _____ lying.

9 I can make a salad. I can set the table.

I can _____ the table.

10 The war will end. More people will die.

The war _____ die.

11 We can work until 6. We can go home now.

We can _____ home now.

COORDINATING CONJUNCTION SO

Presentation

Use *so* to connect two simple sentences when the first sentence is a cause (reason for something) and the second sentence is an effect (result). Place a comma before *so*. Remember that a simple sentence must have a subject and a verb.

Rules	Examples
Use *so* to connect two simple sentences when the first sentence is a cause (reason for something) and the second sentence is an effect (result). Place a comma before *so*.	Ronaldo was born in New York, **so** he is an American citizen.
	My computer is broken, **so** I can't check my email.

Practice 1

Read the sentence. Underline *Correct* or *Incorrect*.

1 It stopped raining so we can go outside. [Correct, Incorrect]

2 My grandfather loves his work, so he does not want to retire. [Correct, Incorrect]

3 Japan does not have oil, so imports oil from other countries. [Correct, Incorrect]

4 Karen loves plants, so she is studying plant biology. [Correct, Incorrect]

5 It's my father's birthday so, I'm going to bake a cake for him. [Correct, Incorrect]

6 Kim doesn't have a car, so she takes the bus to school. [Correct, Incorrect]

7 Juan quit his job, so he has a lot of free time. [Correct, Incorrect]

8 I overslept so, I was late to work. [Correct, Incorrect]

9 Rahim is allergic to milk so he never eats ice cream. [Correct, Incorrect]

10 The book was boring, so returned it to the library. [Correct, Incorrect]

Practice 2

Part 1

Draw lines to match the causes and effects.

1 I'm not hungry.   She is very tired.

2 Mike lost his textbook.   We got lost.

3 Jeff cannot hear well.   He can't do his homework.

4 Sheila has a new baby.   He always sits near the teacher.

5 We got wrong directions to the theater.   I don't want to eat.

Part 2

Combine the sentences you matched. Use *so*. Don't forget the comma.

Example:

1 *I'm* __not hungry, so I don't want to eat__ .

2 Mike _____ .

3 Jeff _____ .

4 Sheila _____ .

5 We _____ .

Subordinating Conjunctions

SUBORDINATING CONJUNCTION IF

We use *if* to write about possibilities in the present, past, and future. Sentences with *if* have two parts, or clauses.

- Both clauses must have a subject and a verb.

- The clause with *if* shows a condition or cause. The main clause shows a result or possible result.

- Use the subordinating conjunction *if* to talk about a present cause or condition and future effect. Use the present tense in the *if*-clause and the future tense in the main clause.

- If you write the clause with *if* at the beginning of the sentence, put a comma after it. If you write the *if*-clause second, do not use a comma.

Examples:

condition result

    With comma: If she studies hard, she will get good grades.

result condition

    Without comma: She will get good grades if she studies hard.

Practice 1

Read the sentences with *if*. Underline *Correct* or *Incorrect*. Pay attention to verb tenses.

1 If it rains tonight, won't go to my dance class. [Correct, Incorrect]

2 If Masako will receive a scholarship, she will go to college in the United States. [Correct, Incorrect]

3 Maria will call her parents if she has time. [Correct, Incorrect]

4 We will have a substitute teacher if our regular teacher sick. [Correct, Incorrect]

5 I will be late, if there is a lot of traffic. [Correct, Incorrect]

6 We go to the beach tomorrow if the weather is nice. [Correct, Incorrect]

7 If I will not understand the grammar lesson, I ask my teacher to explain it again. [Correct, Incorrect]

8 We will go skiing tomorrow if it snows tonight. [Correct, Incorrect]

Practice 2

Combine each pair of sentences to make one sentence with *if*. Don't change the order of the clauses. Add a comma if necessary.

Example:

1 *I will have time. I will go jogging.*

  <u>If I have time, I will go jogging</u> .

2 I will study hard. I will get good grades.

  _____ .

3 I will get a part-time job. I will need money.

  _____ .

4 Joe will get a job. He will buy a car.

  _____ .

5 I will miss you. You will move away.

  _____ .

6 I will get an A on my test. My parents will be proud.

  _____ .

7 You will not answer your phone. I will leave a message.

  _____ .

8 I will walk to work. The weather will be nice.

  _____ .

9 We will be late. The boss will be angry.

  _____ .

SUBORDINATING CONJUNCTION BECAUSE

Presentation

We use *because* to answer the question *Why*? Sentences with *because* have two parts, a reason (or cause) and a result (or effect). *Because* introduces the reason. It can go at the beginning or in the middle of the sentence. For example:

   cause effect

1) Because Mary works 60 hours a week, she doesn't have time for hobbies.

   effect cause

2) Mary doesn't have time for hobbies because she works 60 hours a week.

If you write *because* at the beginning of the sentence, put a comma between the reason and the result. If you write *because* in the middle, do not use a comma.

Practice 1

Read the sentence. Underline *Correct* or *Incorrect*.

1 Nina always takes the stairs because she is afraid of elevators. [Correct, Incorrect]

2 My grandfather does not want to retire, because he loves his work. [Correct, Incorrect]

3 Because Japan does not have oil, it imports oil from other countries. [Correct, Incorrect]

4 We're going to have a party, because it is my mother's birthday. [Correct, Incorrect]

5 Because Lee doesn't have a car, he takes the bus to school. [Correct, Incorrect]

6 Because Juan is a full-time student he doesn't have time to work. [Correct, Incorrect]

7 I went to bed early because I was very tired. [Correct, Incorrect]

8 Chang never eats bread or pasta, because he is allergic to wheat. [Correct, Incorrect]

Practice 2

Combine the following pairs of sentences with *because* at the beginning and in the middle of the sentence.

Example:

1 *We didn't have class. / The teacher was absent.*

  a We didn't have class because the teacher was absent.

  b Because the teacher was absent, we didn't have class.

2 I'm not hungry. / I don't want to eat.

  a Because I'm not hungry _____ .

  b I don't want to eat _____ .

3 Bob and Sheila have a new baby. / They're always tired.

   a Bob and Sheila are always tired _____ .

   b Because Bob and Sheila have a new baby _____ .

4 We were late. / Traffic was very bad.

   a We were late _____ .

   b Because traffic was very bad _____ .

5 My car didn't start. / The battery was dead.

   a My car didn't start _____ .

   b Because the battery was dead _____ .

6 I got 90% on my test. / You helped me study.

   a I got 90% on my test _____ .

   b Because you helped me study _____ .

7 The room was hot. / I opened the window.

   a I opened the window _____ .

   b Because the room was hot _____ .

8 Henry did not laugh. / The joke was not funny.

   a Henry did not laugh _____ .

   b Because the joke was not funny _____ .

9 Barbara eats a lot of fast food. / She doesn't enjoy cooking.

   a Barbara eats a lot of fast food _____ .

   b Because she doesn't enjoy cooking _____ .

SUBORDINATING CONJUNCTIONS BEFORE, AFTER, AND WHEN

Presentation

- *Before*, *after*, and *when* are subordinating conjunctions. We use them in complex sentences.

- Complex sentences have an independent clause and a dependent clause. An independent clause can stand by itself. A dependent clause can't stand by itself, and it begins with a subordinating conjunction. If you write the dependent clause first, put a comma after it. If the main clause is first, don't write a comma.

Follow these rules for using *before*, *after*, and *when*:

Rules	Examples
Before tells you that an event happened earlier than another event.	You should wash your hands **before** you eat. (*You wash your hands first. Then you eat.*)
After tells you that something happened at a later time	**After** I check my email (*first action*), I'll walk the dog (*second action*).
When tells you what time something happens or in what kind of situation it happens. We also use *when* to describe the effect of an action.	I left the house **when** the rain stopped.
	When it stops raining, I'll go outside.
	When the bird sang, the cat meowed.

Practice 1

Read the sentence. Underline the action that happened, or will happen first.

1 Dan will stop working after he is 65.

2 I will eat dinner before I do my homework.

3 Carol will turn 22 after she graduates from college.

4 We will be sad after you leave.

5 Even before the doorbell rang, the dog barked.

6 Before Judy left the office, she called her husband.

7 After he went swimming, Lam felt better.

8 Right after I eat too much, I feel uncomfortable.

9 Just before the sun went down, it got very cold.

10 The passengers clapped after the plane landed.

11 Peter was very lonely before he met his girlfriend.

Practice 2

Combine the two simple sentences into one complex sentence with the subordinator in parentheses. Use a comma if necessary.

Example:

1 *First event: I'm tired.*

Second event: I go to bed early.

(when) <u>When I'm tired, I go to bed early.</u> *OR* <u>I go to bed early when I'm tired.</u>

2 First event: I finish dinner.

Second event: I will wash the dishes.

(after) _____

3 First event: We will eat.

Second event: The chicken is ready.

(when) _____

4 First event: We turn off the lights.

Second event: We go to bed.

(before) _____

5 First event: I went to school.

Second event: I didn't know how to read.

(before) _____

6 First event: The concert ended.

Second event: The musicians left the stage.

(when) _____

7 First event: I eat breakfast.

Second event: I go to work.

(before) _____

8 First event: Chantal graduated from college.

Second event: She went to law school.

(after) _____

9 First event: I stay up late.

Second event: I get tired.

(when) _____

10 First event: Check your test paper.

Second event: You turn it in.

(before) _____

11 First event: Jane sold her house.

Second event: She moved to Florida.

(after) _____

The Sentence

SUBJECT AND VERB

Presentation

English sentences have a **subject** and a **verb**. The subject often comes before the verb. A sentence begins with a capital letter and ends with a form of punctuation: a period, a question mark, an exclamation point.

Rules	Examples
The subject tells who or what does something.	**The mail** arrived.
It can be a noun or pronoun.	**They** will not be at the meeting.
It can be a person, place, thing, or idea.	**Horses** are beautiful animals.
It can have more than one word.	**Gary and Mina** work together.
There are two kinds of verbs. Action verbs (e.g., *walk, laugh, drive*) express an action. Linking (or *stative*) verbs (e.g., *be, seem, look, become, taste, smell*) connect the subject and the rest of the sentence.	George **carried** the baby. The baby **seems** sick.

Practice 1

Circle the letter of the subject of each sentence.

Example:

1 *My aunt and uncle like coffee and tea.*
- **a** *my aunt*
- **b** *my uncle*
- **ⓒ** *my aunt and uncle*

2 The school does not have a library.
- **a** The school
- **b** have
- **c** a library

3 Kate and Anita will speak at the meeting.

  a speak

  b meeting

  c Kate and Anita

4 Every morning, Yang gets out of bed and stretches.

  a morning

  b bed

  c Yang

5 The living room and the dining room are painted blue.

  a The living room

  b The living room and the dining room

  c the dining room

6 The traffic on Canyon Drive is terrible every morning.

  a The traffic

  b Canyon Drive

  c morning

7 We planted roses and lilies in the front garden.

  a garden

  b roses and lilies

  c We

8 The park has picnic tables, benches, and swings.

  a swings

  b picnic tables

  c The park

9 Every family on my street has a dog.

  a dog

  b family

  c street

Practice 2

Read each sentence. If it is correct, circle Correct. If it is incorrect, circle No subject or No verb.

1 My name Roberto. [Correct, No subject, No verb]

2 The capital of South Korea is Seoul. [Correct, No subject, No verb]

3 Seoul big city. [Correct, No subject, No verb]

4 Is more than 2,000 years old. [Correct, No subject, No verb]

5 Our new teacher seems like a nice person. [Correct, No subject, No verb]

6 She very tall. [Correct, No subject, No verb]

7 Drives a green sports car. [Correct, No subject, No verb]

8 Is very cool car. [Correct, No subject, No verb]

9 I want to drive it. [Correct, No subject, No verb]

SUBJECT, VERB, OBJECT

Presentation

- The most common English word order is subject + verb + direct object or complement.

- A direct object comes after an action verb. It receives the action of the verb. Ask yourself: Subject + verb + *who* or *what?* = direct object. For example:

  subject verb object

  The baby is eating a cookie. (The baby is eating *what?*)

- A complement comes after a linking verb. It gives more information about the subject. It can be a noun, pronoun, or adjective. For example:

  subject verb complement (adjective)

  Terry is intelligent.

  subject verb complement (noun)

  Robert is a lawyer.

Practice 1

Underline the direct object or complement in each sentence.

1 Cathy is reading a novel.

2 Quinta practices piano every day.

3 You seem tired today.

4 My dog likes tomatoes.

5 Yo Yo Ma is a famous cello player.

6 Mr. Garza teaches Spanish.

7 Nancy opened the window.

8 Maria is baking a cake.

9 Both of my parents were gymnasts in college.

10 Kelly's major is economics.

11 A long time ago, the United States was a British colony.

Practice 2

Write the words and phrases in the correct order to make sentences.

Example:

1

lost	my	phone	I

<u>I lost my phone</u> .

2

speaks	three languages	Chandra

_____ .

3

my car	A mechanic	fixed

_____ .

4

plays	the trumpet	Wynton Marsalis

_____ .

5

is	very quiet	Katya's boyfriend

_____ .

6

is	boring	Joyce's job

_____ .

7

our compositions	Professor Baker	corrected

_____ .

8

| doesn't have | a smart phone | Jackie |

_____ .

9

| is | A pediatrician | a doctor for children |

_____ .

10

| his sister's friend | Serdar | married |

_____ .

RUN-ON SENTENCES

Presentation

A run-on sentence is a writing mistake. It happens when you do not connect your sentences correctly. There are several kinds of run-on sentences.

Run-on sentence	*My name is Cristina I am from Brazil.*
Problem	There is no connecting word or punctuation between the sentences.
How to correct	Add a comma + *and*: *My name is Cristina, and I am from Brazil.* Note: Adding just a comma does not fix the run-on sentence.
Run-on sentence	*I will finish my homework, after I will go to bed.*
Problem	*After* is used incorrectly.
How to correct	a) Write a compound sentence: *I will finish my homework, and then I will go to bed.* b) Write a time clause with *after*: *After I finish my homework, I will go to bed.*
Run-on sentence	*I graduated from college, I went to work.*
Problem	There is no connecting word between the sentences.
How to correct	Start a new sentence: *I graduated from college. I went to work.*
Run-on sentence	*I hate my apartment, I'm going to move.*
Problem	A comma cannot separate two sentences.
How to correct	a) Replace the comma with a period: *I hate my apartment. I'm going to move.* b) Add a coordinating conjunction: *I hate my apartment, so I'm going to move.*

Practice 1

Underline **Run-on** if a sentence is a run-on sentence. Choose **OK** if a sentence is correct.

Example:

1 *I will finish my homework, after I will go to bed. [<u>Run-on</u>, OK]*

2 I live in Addis Ababa it is the capital of Ethiopia. [Run-on, OK]

3 The plane landed, then everybody clapped. [Run-on, OK]

4 I'm going to call the doctor's office. My son has a high fever. [Run-on, OK]

5 I feel sad today, I miss my parents. [Run-on, OK]

6 I'm going to finish the housework, after I will pick up the kids at school. [Run-on, OK]

7 I don't own a car, I plan to buy one next year. [Run-on, OK]

8 We checked in to the hotel, then we went up to our room. [Run-on, OK]

9 Joyce played a game of tennis. After that, she swam for half an hour. [Run-on, OK]

Practice 2

Read the paragraphs. Underline six run-on sentences.

Paragraph 1

I had a bad morning, everything went wrong. First I overslept, and then I slipped in the shower. I cut myself shaving, I burned my breakfast. I was late to work, and my boss was angry at me. I hope tomorrow will be better it can't be worse!

Paragraph 2

I'm going to graduate from New York University in 2015 then I will return to my country. I plan to work for my father. He has a software company in Seoul. I will work there for two or three years, and then I will return to the United States. I want to get an MBA degree after I can manage my father's company. I will manage the company my father will retire.

SUBJECT-VERB AGREEMENT

Presentation

In an English sentence, the subject and verb must agree. This means that a singular subject needs a singular verb. A plural subject needs a plural verb:

Singular subject + singular verb: The teacher is late.

Plural subject + plural verb: The teachers are in a meeting.

Rules	Examples
Noncount nouns are singular and take singular verbs.	The **homework was** difficult.
	The **milk tastes** sour.
In noun phrases such as *all of the boys*, *some of the work*, *most of the words*, and *a lot of the time*, the verb agrees with the noun. It does not agree with *all*, *some*, or *a lot*.	All of the **boys are** wearing uniforms.
	Some of the **information was** wrong.
If there are words between the subject and the verb, then make sure the subject and verb agree.	The **vase** on the table **is** very old.
	The **students** in the dormitory **are** good friends.
Compound subjects take plural verbs.	**The president and his wife are** standing by the window.

Practice 1

Underline the verb that matches the subject in each sentence.

Example:

1 *The dirty clothes on the floor [is, are] Jack's.*
2 The air in the room [smell, smells] bad.
3 Most of the work [is, are] finished.
4 Tigers [is, are] good swimmers.
5 The living room and the dining room [is, are] very cold.
6 Some of the grass [is, are] brown.
7 My brother Robert [drive, drives] too fast.

8 Many teenagers [drive, drives] too fast.

9 The weather [is, are] going to be bad all week.

10 The music [sound, sounds] beautiful.

11 The musicians [is, are] very talented.

Practice 2

Complete each sentence with the singular or plural form of the verb in parentheses.

Example:

1 *The names __are__ (be) hard to pronounce.*

2 My hand _____ (hurt) from typing all day.

3 All the students _____ (know) the answer.

4 The printer on the third floor _____ (be) not working.

5 Loud music _____ (give) me a headache.

6 The boys _____ (need) a haircut.

7 Bears, sharks, and snakes _____ (have) an excellent sense of smell.

8 All the houses on my block _____ (have) porches.

9 Transportation in my city _____ (be) fast and convenient.

10 The gardener _____ (come) every Tuesday.

11 All of my work _____ (be) finished.

Parts of Speech

COMMON AND PROPER NOUNS

Presentation

A *noun* can be a person, place, thing, or idea. In a sentence, a noun can be the subject, object, indirect object, or object of the preposition. There are two groups of nouns: proper nouns and common nouns.

Rules	Examples
Proper nouns begin with capital letters. They can be plural or singular. They name specific, unique people, places, ideas, or things.	Let's dine with the **Asquiths** tonight
	My roommate's name is **Paul Jones**. *(person)*
	I was in **Houston, Texas** last month. *(place)*
	Where are you going for **Thanksgiving**? *(thing)*
	She's taking a class on **Surrealism**. *(idea)*
Common nouns do not begin with capital letters. They can be count or noncount. They usually refer to a general class of things.	My **teacher** speaks Chinese very well. *(person)*
	Let's go to the **mall**. *(place)*
	Can I borrow your **car**? *(thing)*
	I need more **time**. *(idea)*

Practice 1

Underline 12 common nouns in the following paragraph.

Hawaii is my favorite place for a vacation. My sister and her family live on the island of Maui. I go there almost every December. In Hawaii I can go to the beach and enjoy the warm sun on Christmas day. My home is in Philadelphia. It is very cold there in the winter. My friends are jealous when I return from Hawaii with a tan.

Practice 2

Underline 10 proper nouns in the following paragraphs.

My cousin, Anna, is a university student in Chicago. Her major is art history. She is interested in modern art. Her favorite painter is Picasso. He was the founder of a style of painting called Cubism.

Last year, my cousin had a wonderful experience. She studied in Paris, France, for one semester. While she was there, she visited the Louvre and other famous museums. She also traveled to Madrid. She wanted to see Picasso's most famous painting, the Guernica. It is at a museum there.

VERBS

Presentation

In English, there are action verbs and non-action verbs. In a statement, the verb usually comes after the subject.

Rules	Examples
Action verbs describe a sensation, movement, or an action.	Jack **drives** a sports car.
	Cows **eat** grass.
Non-action verbs do not describe actions. They describe feelings, conditions, or states.	The flowers **smell** good.
	The mail **is** late.
	Jennifer **has** a cold.

Practice 1

Underline the verb in each sentence.

1 I live in a nice apartment building.

2 My apartment is small.

3 It has one big room, a bathroom, and a tiny kitchen.

4 My neighbors, Katya and Ilan, are very friendly.

5 I like them very much.

6 We eat dinner together once or twice a week.

7 Sometimes we watch television together.

8 They have a baby boy.

9 I babysit for them every Sunday night.

10 They help me, too.

Practice 2

Read the sentence. Underline Correct if the verb is in the correct place, and Incorrect if it is not.

1 Shira in San Diego lives. [Correct, Incorrect]

2 Shira my friend is. [Correct, Incorrect]

3 Her name means "song" in Hebrew. [Correct, Incorrect]

4 Likes Shira to write. [Correct, Incorrect]

5 She writes for the college newspaper. [Correct, Incorrect]

6 Has she also an Internet blog. [Correct, Incorrect]

7 Shira likes to stay busy. [Correct, Incorrect]

8 At the community center, takes she a creative writing class. [Correct, Incorrect]

9 She always finds time to hang out with friends, too. [Correct, Incorrect]

ADJECTIVES

Adjectives describe nouns or pronouns.

Rules	Examples
Adjectives come before nouns.	**expensive** shoes, a **friendly** neighbor
Adjectives come after forms of *be* and some non-action verbs.	He is **tall**.
	You look **great**.
Articles (*a, an, the*), possessives (*my, your,* etc.), and numbers are types of adjectives.	**a** party, **his** guitar, **two** cookies
Adjectives have only one form. They never have an *-s* ending.	Incorrect: beautifuls girls
	Correct: **beautiful** girls
Adjectives come between articles and nouns and between possessives and nouns	my **favorite** restaurant, the **hot** soup
You can use two or more adjectives together.	an **old, yellow** car; a **long, black** dress
Nouns can be adjectives if they come before another noun.	a **school** uniform, a **computer** program

Practice 1

Underline ten adjectives in the paragraph.

Josie's is a small coffee shop near my house. I go there when I am tired or bored. It is a nice place to take a break. It has comfortable tables and chairs, and the coffee is delicious. It smells wonderful. At Josie's I can meet friendly people, and I can hear interesting conversations.

Practice 2

Circle the letter of the sentence that is correct.

1 a It is today hot.
  b It is hot today.

2 a I love cherry tomatoes.
  b I love tomatoes cherry.

3 a It also has food Mexican.
  b It also has Mexican food.

4 a I ate there night last.
  b I ate there last night.

5 a I ordered a burrito vegetarian.
  b I ordered a vegetarian burrito.

6 a Mrs. Sarkis cooks food Greek.
  b Mrs. Sarkis cooks Greek food.

7 a There is a new restaurant near our house.
  b There is a restaurant new near our house.

8 a I lost my favorite jeans.
  b I lost my jeans favorite.

9 a Yoshi has sixteen pairs of shoes.
  b Yoshi has pairs of sixteen shoes.

10 a Don't walk on the floor wet.
  b Don't walk on the wet floor.

PARAGRAPH ORGANIZATION

Topic Sentence

Topic Sentence

The topic sentence is usually the first sentence of a paragraph. It gives the writer's main idea. All the sentences in the paragraph are about this main idea.

A topic sentence has two parts:

The **topic:** What the paragraph is about

The **controlling idea:** What the sentences in the paragraph will discuss or explain about the topic

There are two ways to write a topic sentence. You can write the topic first, or you can write the controlling idea first. For example:

> I love gardening for three reasons.

> There are three reasons why I love gardening.

> *gardening:* topic

> *three reasons:* controlling idea

Practice 1

Read the topic sentence. Circle the controlling idea in each sentence.

1 I respect my parents because they are generous and hardworking.

2 My favorite jeans are fashionable and comfortable.

3 Calcium is important for strong bones and teeth.

4 There are two kinds of coffee beans, "Arabica" and "robusta."

5 Because they eat insects, bats are very important and useful animals.

6 Many champion swimmers have long arms and big feet.

7 Peanuts are not "true" nuts.

8 The perfect place to go for a winter vacation is Cozumel, Mexico.

9 It's easy and fun to grow tomatoes in pots.

10 High heels are very bad for your feet and legs.

11 I'm going to tell you two important facts about buying a new car.

Practice 2

Read each paragraph and circle the letter for the best topic sentence.

1 _____ First, it is the color of the sun. I feel warm when I wear yellow clothes, especially in the winter. Second, yellow is a cheerful color. When I'm tired or worried, yellow flowers or a yellow jacket make me happy. Finally, yellow reminds me of my grandmother. She died two years ago. Yellow was her favorite color, too. When I see a yellow car or a yellow house, I think of my grandmother and remember her love.

a I have a lot of yellow clothes.

b I love the color yellow for several reasons.

c Yellow is a very happy color.

2 _____ Many bats eat fruit. They help pollinate plants and spread seeds. Bats also help control insects. They eat huge numbers of insects, including insects that damage crops. For example, a brown bat can eat more than one thousand insects the size of a mosquito in one hour. A report in *Science* magazine says bats save American farmers billions of dollars every year by reducing crop damage and limiting the need for chemicals that kill insects.

a Bats are found in many parts of the world.

b Bats are important for agriculture and our environment.

c There are more than 1,200 kinds of bats.

3 _____ It is yellow or green on the outside and white on the inside. It has a very thick rind ("skin"). It is the largest citrus fruit—15 to 25 centimeters in diameter—and weighs between 1 and 2 kilos. It tastes like a sweet grapefruit. For that reason, it is a popular dessert in some Southeast Asian countries. In China, some people use the leaves in their bath. In Malaysia, people use the fruit as a decoration. And in Assam, India, children often use it as a football!

a A pomelo is a large citrus fruit with a number of interesting uses.

b *Citrus Maxima* is the Latin name of the pomelo.

c The pomelo is native to Southeast Asia.

Ordering

TIME ORDER

Presentation

Time Order

Time order means you organize the sentences of a paragraph from the earliest event to the latest. There are two kinds of time-order paragraphs: narrative and process. A **narrative** is an event, story, or experience. A **process** describes how to do or make something. Both types of paragraphs use **topic sentences**. A topic sentence tells you what the main idea of the paragraph is.

Compare the topic sentences for a narrative paragraph and a process paragraph:

- Narrative: *Mr. and Mrs. Kana have a daily routine at their small grocery store.*
- Process: *To make a great cup of coffee, follow these steps.*

Time-order paragraphs use time-order words and phrases to make the order clear.

Use a comma after time-order words except *then*. Don't use a comma after *then*.

Example:

> **First,** I boil some water. **Then** I put rice in it.

Time-Order Words	Examples
first, second, third	*(Narrative)* **First**, Mr. Kana turns on the lights. **Next**, he turns on the computer.
to begin, to start	
next, then, after that, later	*(Process)* **To begin**, pour water into the coffee maker. **After that**, measure the coffee. **Finally**, pour a little milk into the black coffee. **After dinner**, rinse the dishes right away.
finally, last	
after, before	

Practice 1

Complete each paragraph. Write the correct word or phrase to complete the sentence.

Next	Finally	To begin
Second	Third	

Paragraph 1

Last week I traveled from my house in Los Angeles to my sister's house in San Diego without using my car. _____ , I left my house and walked to the bus stop. That took about ten minutes. _____ , I took the bus to the subway station about 2 miles away. _____ , I took the subway to the train station downtown. _____ , I took the Amtrak train to downtown San Diego. _____ , I walked from the train station to my sister's house. My whole trip took about four hours. It was fun!

Last	Then	To begin	Third

Paragraph 2

You can use baking soda to remove stains from your stove. _____ , pour a little boiling water on the stain. _____ take a teaspoon of baking soda and put it on the stain. Let it sit for about a minute. _____ , take a soft cloth and rub the baking soda around the stain. You will see the stain disappear like magic! _____ , wipe away the water and baking soda. If you use baking soda, you don't need to use strong chemicals, and you will not scratch your stove.

Practice 2

Number each sentence from 1 to 6 in the correct time order.

Paragraph 1

I am going to tell you how to make hiccups go away.

_____ Second, take a deep breath and hold it.

_____ After you take the first sip, drink some more small sips for 20 or 30 seconds. Be sure to hold your breath the whole time.

_____ Finally, stand up and breathe out. Your hiccups will be gone.

_____ First, fill a tall glass with water.

_____ Next, take a small sip of water from the far side of the glass. If you sip from the far side, the water will not spill.

_____ Third, bend over and hold the glass of water under your mouth.

Paragraph 2

Sunday is a relaxing day for my teacher, Mr. White. He usually gets up around 8:30 in the morning.

_____ After he reads, he works in his garden for one or two hours.

_____ Next, he has breakfast and reads the newspaper.

_____ Later in the day, he goes shopping, visits his parents, or goes to the movie with a friend.

_____ Finally, he comes home and gets ready for work the next day.

_____ Then he goes back inside and eats lunch.

_____ First, he takes a shower and shaves.

LISTING ORDER

Listing Order

One way to organize a paragraph is by listing the details that support the topic sentence. In listing-order paragraphs, the topic sentence always includes a number or quantity word.

Example: *There are two kinds of elephants: African and Asian.*

You may choose to list the details in any order, or you may decide to put the most important detail at the beginning or end.

Here are some listing-order words and phrases. Notice the commas.

Words and Phrases	Examples
first, first of all	I want to accomplish four goals in the next five years. **First of all**, I plan to graduate from a university. **Second**, I would like to find a good job. **In addition**, I would like to buy an apartment. **Most importantly**, I hope to find a kind, smart, and independent woman to marry.
second, third, fourth, etc.	
in addition, also	
finally, last, most important(ly)	

Practice 1

Read each topic sentence. Underline the sentence if it shows that the paragraph will use listing order.

There are three reasons why I want to be a nurse.

The nursing program at State College is very difficult.

Follow these few suggestions to save money on your monthly water bill.

Riding my bicycle to work has several advantages.

The state of California does not have enough teachers.

My doctor's office is a comfortable place to wait.

There are three easy things you can do to lower your blood pressure.

There are three reasons why I do not have a smart phone.

A good teacher needs to have four important qualities.

George Washington, the first U.S. president, had a fascinating life.

Practice 2

Complete each paragraph. Write the correct word or phrase to complete the sentence.

Finally,	First of all,	Second,	In addition,

Paragraph 1

Owning a pet has several important advantages. _____ pets are good companions. You can talk to them. If you live alone, having a pet can help you feel less lonely. _____ pets help to reduce stress. Touching a pet can make your blood pressure go down. That's why it is healthy for older people to have a cat or dog. _____ pets can make your home safer. For example, most dogs bark when a stranger comes to your door. If there is a fire, a cat can wake you up by moving around. _____ pets are healthy for children. Children with pets have fewer allergies than children without pets.

Also,	Most important,	First,

Paragraph 2

My exercise teacher, Sofia, has three excellent qualities. _____ she is creative. She has special classes for many different ages and ability levels. For example, she teaches a special exercise class for people in wheelchairs. _____ Sofia is patient. She smiles and encourages us, especially when we are tired or slow. This makes everybody try harder. _____ Sofia cares about safety. She doesn't push anyone too hard, and she makes sure we take regular breaks and drink lots of water. Sofia is my favorite aerobics teacher because of these qualities.

| Also, | Last, | Third, | For one thing, |

Paragraph 3

My cousin Annabelle has many bad driving habits. _____ she always talks on her cell phone while she drives. This is illegal, but Annabelle doesn't care. She thinks the law is "stupid." _____ Annabelle likes to eat and drink while she drives. This means she only has one hand on the steering wheel. It's not safe. _____ she rolls through stop signs instead of stopping completely. One time she almost hit some children. _____ Annabelle drives too fast. She gets angry if I tell her to slow down. I think Annabelle needs to take a driver's education class.

SPACE ORDER

Presentation

Space Order

When you describe a place, you can use space order to organize the details.

Examples:

left to right / right to left

top to bottom / bottom to top

front to back / back to front

outside to inside / inside to outside

east to west / west to east

north to south / south to north

near to far / far to near

The topic sentence for a space-order paragraph should

- mention the space you are describing
- make a comment about it

Use *There is / There are* and prepositions of location to say where things are.

Practice 1

Read each paragraph. Circle the letter of the space order in each one.

1 The continental United States has four time zones. The first zone in the West is called the Pacific zone. It includes the states next to the Pacific Ocean, plus Nevada. The Mountain time zone is east of the Pacific zone. It is one hour later. It includes the Rocky Mountain states, such as Colorado and Montana. Moving east we have the Central time zone. It includes all the Great Plains and Southern states, for example, Iowa, Texas, and Alabama. This zone is two hours later than the Pacific zone. The fourth time

zone is called Eastern. It includes the states next to the Atlantic Ocean, such as New York and Florida. There is a three-hour difference between the Pacific and Eastern time zones.

a right to left

b west to east

c front to back

2 My veterinarian's office is well-organized. When you enter, you come into a waiting area with chairs and sofas. The receptionist's desk is opposite the entrance, on the far side of the waiting room. Behind the desk there is a door, and behind the door there is a hall with rooms on both sides. First, there are examination rooms where the veterinarian examines pets. Down the hall there is an operating room. Finally, at the end of the hall, there is a restroom and the doctor's office.

a right to left

b far to near

c front to back

3 The dining room in my house is large and comfortable. It is about 12 feet square. In the center there is a big, square table. Around the table there are eight chairs. There is art on the walls around the room. On the east and south walls there are large windows. They allow light to enter the room all day. On the west wall there is a large cabinet for dishes. There is also a door leading to the kitchen. Finally, on the north wall, there is an arch that connects the dining room to the living room. The dining room is painted a soft, sand color. It is a very relaxing room.

a right to left

b inside to outside

c front to back

Practice 2

Read each paragraph. Circle the letter of the best topic sentence.

1 _____ .

Washington is next to Canada. It has 71,300 square miles and almost 7 million people. It gets an average of 39 inches of rain a year. South of Washington is the state of Oregon, with an area of about 98,000 square miles but only about 4 million people. Oregon has 27 inches of rain each year. South of Oregon is California. It has 163,696 square miles and 38 million people. California gets an average of about 22 inches of rain each year.

a A driving trip from California to Washington can be a fantastic vacation.

b From north to south, the Pacific states are Washington, Oregon, and California.

c California has the best weather of any U.S. state.

2 _____ . It is shaped like a rectangle, and it has one door in the middle of the front of the house. When you enter the door, you see a long hallway with three doors on each side. Usually one family lives in each of these six rooms. This means there are often from fifteen to twenty five people living in the house. At the back of the house there is a common area for cooking. There is also a toilet and an area for bathing.

  a In Tanzania, a common style of house is the Swahili house.

  b Tanzania is a country in east-central Africa on the Indian Ocean.

  c Swahili is the official language of Kenya and Tanzania.

3 _____ . St. Paul's church was built more than 150 years ago. It is the oldest building in town, and it is still in use. Next to the church is the Grove Theater. Members of the community perform plays there several times a year. Down the street on the right is the fire station. It has a museum with many old photographs and an old fire engine. At the end of the street there is one more interesting building, Sam's Diner. This popular restaurant was built in the 1950s in the Art Deco style. Tourists enjoy taking pictures of it. These four buildings give Pine Avenue an interesting character.

  a The Art Deco style of architecture was popular in the 1950s.

  b Small towns often have interesting architecture.

  c There are a number of interesting old buildings on Pine Avenue, my town's main street.

Supporting Sentences
PROVIDING REASONS

Presentation

Providing Reasons

Reasons answer the question *Why?* For example, you can give reasons to explain why you like something or did something.

You can organize your paragraph of reasons like this:

Topic sentence

Reason 1

Reason 2

Reason 3

Conclusion

Here are some common ways to write a topic sentence for a reason paragraph:

- There are several reasons I like …
- There are three reasons I don't like …
- I like _____ for three reasons.
- I don't like _____ because …

Your conclusion can repeat the main idea with the same or similar words. You can also give your opinion or a final comment.

If you have more than one reason, you can connect them with these transitions:

Examples		
First,	Second,	Finally,
First of all,	Also,	My last reason is….
To begin,	Another reason is….	One reason is….
My first reason is….		

Practice 1

Write in the correct transition in each paragraph on the next page.

Finally	Second	Also	First of all

Paragraph 1

There are several reasons why autumn is my favorite season in Southern California. _____ , I love the cool air. It feels wonderful to walk outside after the long, hot summer. _____ , I love the rain. It never rains here in the summer, so the first rains of autumn are very welcome. _____ , I like autumn because I enjoy wearing scarves and wool sweaters. They are soft and comfortable on my skin. _____ , I love autumn because I can work in my garden. I can plant flowers now, and they will bloom in the spring. These are the reasons why I look forward to autumn every year.

Another reason is	One reason is	The third reason is

Paragraph 2

There are three reasons why my family doesn't go to movie theaters anymore. _____ the price. A movie ticket in our area costs $14. I think that's too much. _____ that many people in the theater are rude. They talk during the movie, and they send text messages. It's hard to concentrate. _____ that movies these days are too loud. The sound hurts our ears. For all these reasons, my family prefers to watch movies at home.

Second	First of all	Last	Another reason

Paragraph 3

I really like my aerobics teacher, Cassie, for three reasons. _____ , I like her exercise routines. She creates new routines for every class, so her classes are never boring. _____ , she picks great music. It's fun to move to the songs she picks. _____ I like Cassie is that she always encourages us. Her words give me the energy to keep moving, even if I'm tired. _____ , Cassie is a great role model. She is strong, and she looks really healthy. She is a good example for us. In conclusion, I love my exercise classes with Cassie, and I don't want to exercise with anyone else.

Practice 2

Number the sentences in the correct order to make a paragraph.

Paragraph 1

____ Also, I don't need a smartphone. I work at home, and I don't go out very much. I can use my computer to get information or check my email.

____ First of all, smartphones are expensive. The phone is more than $200, and the monthly service plan is very expensive. I can't afford it.

____ Finally, I don't have a smartphone because I am lazy. I don't enjoy learning about new technology. I have a cell phone, a laptop computer, a camera, an iPod, and an ebook reader. That's enough technology for me!

___ There are three reasons why I don't own a smartphone.

___ I hope now you understand why I don't want and don't need a smartphone.

Paragraph 2

___ The third reason I love swimming is that the water feels good. It is cool and clean. It makes my skin feel smooth.

___ The first reason is that swimming is a gentle sport. There is no running or jumping, so I cannot hurt myself when I swim.

___ I love swimming for four reasons.

___ Finally, I love swimming because it is a quiet sport. There is almost no noise in the pool. It's my favorite place to think.

___ Second, swimming is good for my muscles. It is especially good for stretching my back and shoulders. Because I swim, I never have pain in my back.

___ All these reasons explain why swimming is my favorite sport.

USING DETAILS

Presentation

Using Details

Details are also called *supporting sentences* or *body sentences*. They are the sentences that come after the topic sentence.

- Details tell *who, what, when, where, why, how, how much,* or *how many*.
- All the details in a paragraph need to give information about the main idea in the topic sentence.
- Facts, examples, and reasons are three types of details.

Type of Detail	Supporting Sentences
Fact	*(From a paragraph about the Fourth of July)* On the Fourth of July, Americans celebrate the birth of the United States in 1776.
Example	*(From a paragraph about wild animals in the city)* You can often see coyotes walking on the streets of my city.
Reasons	*(From a paragraph explaining why the writer rides his bicycle to work)* One reason I ride my bicycle to work is because I never have to stop in traffic jams.

Practice 1

Read the topic sentence and details. For each item, circle the letter of the sentence that does *not* support the main idea of the paragraph.

1 Topic sentence: Louis Braille (Jan. 4, 1809–Jan. 6, 1852) invented a system to help blind people read.

    a Louis Braille is buried in Paris.

    b He was a teenager when he invented his system.

    c In 1829, Braille published a book about his method.

    d His method, called Braille, is still in use around the world today.

    e It consists of raised dots that blind people can feel with their fingers.

2 Topic sentence: My cousin Helen is a terrible driver.

    a She talks on her cell phone while she drives.

    b She doesn't stop at stop signs.

    c She has a dirty old Toyota.

    d She doesn't use her turn signal when she turns left or right.

    e She drinks coffee while she's driving.

3 Topic sentence: Cats make wonderful pets.

    a They are quiet, beautiful, and very clean.

    b You can leave them alone for a long time.

    c Some people are allergic to cats.

    d Most cats are loving and friendly.

    e It's fun to watch television with my cat on my lap.

Practice 2

Read the topic sentence. Circle the letters of three sentences that support the main idea.

1 Topic sentence: Broccoli is a very healthy vegetable.

    a One cup of broccoli contains all the vitamin C you need in a day.

    b Broccoli helps your digestive system work properly.

    c Broccoli is a plant in the cabbage family.

    d Broccoli helps the body to fight cancer.

    e Some people say that broccoli doesn't taste good.

2 Topic sentence: Kangaroos live in large family groups called "mobs."

    a A mob can have 100 males, females, and babies.

    b Kangaroos are mammals.

    c The head of the mob is the largest male in the group.

    d There are 47 species of kangaroos.

    e The mob gives protection to old, young, and weak animals.

3 Topic sentence: Mary and Jack have an excellent marriage.

   a They make important decisions together.
   b Each of them tries hard to make the other one happy.
   c They were married on April 13, 2008.
   d They respect each other's differences.
   e Last year they bought a small house.

GIVING EXAMPLES

Giving Examples

Examples are a good way to make your ideas clear. An example can support your topic sentence, or it can make a supporting detail stronger.

Examples:

   Topic sentence: My friend Ari enjoys every kind of outdoor sport.

   Example: For example, he loves playing basketball with his friends.

   Topic sentence: My friend Susanna can cook many kinds of ethnic food.

   Supporting detail: First of all, she makes great Mexican food.

   Example: For example, she knows how to prepare delicious fish tacos.

You can use the transition phrases *For instance* or *For example* to introduce examples. Put a comma and a complete sentence after these phrases. You can also write an example without a transition phrase.

Transitions	Examples
for example	I wear different kinds of shoes for different activities. **For example**, I wear running shoes for jogging.
for instance	A number of famous singers are blind. **For instance**, Stevie Wonder cannot see, but he is a wonderful singer and piano player.

Practice 1

Read the topic sentence. Circle the letter of the example that does not support the topic sentence.

1 My grandmother never wastes money.
  a She never recycles plastic bags.
  b She buys all her clothes on sale.
  c She uses coupons when she shops at the supermarket.

2 Doreen has several interesting hobbies.
  a She takes a belly dancing class once a week.
  b She loves to read and collect cookbooks.
  c She is very busy with all her hobbies.

3 Several human foods are dangerous for dogs.
  a Grapes and raisins can hurt a dog's kidneys.
  b It's fine to give your dog slices of apple.
  c Onions and garlic can destroy a dog's red blood cells.

4 It's easy to save electricity in your home.
  a The average home has more than 20 large and small appliances that use electricity.
  b Turn off lights when you're not in a room.
  c Hang your clothes to dry instead of using your clothes dryer.

5 The color of a room may change the way you feel.
  a A red room makes some people feel irritable.
  b Orange makes people hungry, so it is a good color for restaurants.
  c My bedroom is blue and white.

Practice 2

Complete the sentence, using the example in parentheses and *For instance* or *For example* + a comma.

1 *(She loves tomatoes.) My cat likes to eat vegetables.*
  For example, *she loves tomatoes.*

2 (She eats leftover pizza for breakfast) Cindy has unusual eating habits.
  _____ pizza for breakfast.

3 (It tells me the weather in any city.) My new phone does amazing things.
  _____ in any city.

4 (He volunteers at a children's hospital every Saturday.) My friend Ahmed is very kind.
  _____ hospital every Saturday.

5 (Chinese verbs don't have tense.) Chinese grammar is simpler than English grammar.
_____ don't have tense.

6 (Two lily leaves can kill a cat) Some common plants are poisonous.
_____ can kill a cat.

7 (Every Sunday she makes a huge pot of soup.) Akiko manages her time very well.
_____ a huge pot of soup.

8 (He often locks his keys in his car.) Mr. Franklin is very forgetful.
_____ his keys in his car.

9 (He never forgets his wife's birthday.) Stanley Gold is a thoughtful husband.
_____ his wife's birthday.

10 (You can use it to remove stains on your stove.) There are many uses for baking soda.
_____ to remove stains on your stove.

11 (She speaks four languages.) My friend Rihanna is extremely talented.
_____ four languages.

The Conclusion

Practice 1

Read the topic sentence. Circle the letter for the best concluding sentence.

Example:

Topic sentence: *My best friend, Lisa, is generous, kind, and funny.*

Concluding sentence:

a *I am lucky to have a lot of kind and generous friends.*

(b) *I feel lucky to have a good person like Lisa as my best friend.*

c *Lisa and I enjoy shopping and going out together.*

1 Topic sentence: When I go to work, I prefer to take the train.
   Concluding sentence:

   a On the other hand, the train is very crowded after work in the evening.
   b In conclusion, I enjoy talking to people on the train to and from work.
   c These are the reasons why I prefer traveling to work by train.

2 Topic sentence: My hometown, Oceanside, is a wonderful place to live and work.
   Concluding sentence:

   a These reasons explain why I am planning to leave Oceanside and move to a big city.
   b Since it is safe, convenient, and beautiful, I'm glad I live in Oceanside.
   c Oceanside has nice restaurants and good schools.

3 Topic sentence: Coffee tastes good, but did you know it is also good for your health?
   Concluding sentence:

   a However, coffee makes some people nervous.
   b So enjoy your morning cup of coffee—it's good for you!
   c In conclusion, coffee is one of the most popular drinks in the world.

Practice 2

Read each paragraph. Then circle the letter for the best concluding sentence.

1 Hummus is one of the most popular foods in my country, Jordan. We eat it at almost every meal. To make hummus, we mix ground chickpeas (which also has another name, garbanzo beans) with olive oil, lemon juice, and garlic. It makes a thick paste. We eat hummus with a special bread called pita. We can tear off a piece of pita and use it instead of a fork to scoop up some hummus. We can also put the hummus inside the pita with salad or meat and eat it like a sandwich. Hummus is cheap, delicious, and very healthy, too. _____

   a These reasons explain why Jordanian people love hummus.

   b In conclusion, it's easy to learn how to make hummus.

   c Hummus is also popular in Greece, Turkey, and Israel.

2 My friends Michelle and Eric have a very special son. His name is Danny. When Danny was six months old, he had a disease called chicken pox. The disease damaged his brain. Today Danny is 17 years old. He goes to a special school. It's hard for him to walk, talk, and use his hands. He can't read or write. However, Danny is a happy boy. He likes to hug people. He loves music, hot dogs, cats, and animated movies. He has a loud, happy laugh. I enjoy visiting Danny. _____

   a He will never have a job.

   b He has wonderful parents.

   c He is a special person and my special friend.

3 I always travel with three things: ear plugs, swim goggles, and a photo of my dog. I don't like noise, and the ear plugs help me sleep in noisy places like airplanes and hotels on busy streets. I travel with swim goggles because I love to swim. I try to go swimming in every town I visit. Finally, the photo of my dog makes me smile when I am lonely. _____

   a These three objects help me relax and feel at home when I travel.

   b In conclusion, traveling is fun, but I often miss my dog.

   c My dog is like a member of my family.

Unity

Unity

Good paragraphs have **unity**. This means all the sentences in the paragraph support the topic sentence. To check your paragraph for unity, ask these questions:

- What is my topic?
- What is my controlling idea?
- Do all the sentences in my paragraph talk about this topic and this controlling idea?

Example:

In this example, the fifth sentence is not related to the topic of the paragraph ("protect your skin") or the controlling idea ("steps"). The paragraph is not unified.

1) If you have light skin, you need to take special steps to protect your skin from the sun. 2) First, you should always wear sunscreen outdoors, even if the day is cloudy. 3) Be sure to put on more sunscreen every two hours. 4) Next, wear a hat because you can get sunburned under your hair. 5) My grandfather never wore a hat, and he got skin cancer. 6) Third, wear a long-sleeved shirt and long pants. 7) If you follow these steps, your skin will be healthy and young-looking.

Practice 1

For each paragraph, circle the letter of the sentence you can add to make a unified paragraph.

1 My grandmother is 92 years old, but she is still active and healthy. Every day she reads, plays word games, or watches movies in French. To stay strong, she swims and walks. She also has a young spirit. She likes to tell jokes. My grandmother is old, but she loves life.

   a My grandmother was born in New York City in 1920.
   b She has trouble hearing.
   c She enjoys writing emails to her grandchildren.

2 If you live in a dry area, it is easy to save water both inside and outside your house. Inside the house, be sure to fix dripping faucets. Take short showers. Outside the house, water your garden in the early morning when it's cool. If possible, take out your grass and replace it with low-water plants.

   a Many people pay too much for water.
   b Turn off the water while you brush your teeth.
   c Use your towels again if you're staying at a hotel.

Copyright © 2017 by Pearson Education, Inc. Duplication is not permitted.

3 The Dead Sea is a low, salty lake between Israel and Jordan. It is 420 meters below sea level, and the water is 330 meters deep. The Dead Sea is 30% salt. This means it is 8.6 times saltier than the ocean. If you go into the water, you cannot swim. You can only float!

    a Because of the salt, animals cannot live in the Dead Sea.

    b There are luxury hotels on the shores of the Dead Sea.

    c The Dead Sea is famous for its black mud.

Practice 2

Read each paragraph. Underline the sentence that does not belong.

1 London, England, has a temperate climate. This means it is not very cold or very hot. The average winter temperature is about 47 degrees Fahrenheit. Most winters it snows only four or five times. The average summer temperature is a pleasant 73 degrees, and there is not much rain. Summer is the busy tourist season in London. Spring and fall are beautiful, with comfortable temperatures and some rain.

2 There are many kinds of corn. Flint corn grows in Central and South America. It has many colors. It is very hard, so most people do not eat it. Columbus introduced corn to Europe. Dent corn is white or yellow. It is used for feeding animals. It is also used in many industrial products. Sweet corn has more sugar than other kinds of corn. You can buy it fresh, frozen, or canned. Finally, popcorn is a kind of flint corn. It is hard on the outside but soft on the inside. The kernels explode when you heat them. People enjoy eating popcorn in movie theaters.

3 Cellist Yo-Yo Ma is one of the most talented and famous musicians in the world. He plays in many different musical styles, including classical, jazz, country, and traditional Chinese folk music. He also played the cello in the movies *Crouching Tiger, Hidden Dragon,* and *Seven Years in Tibet.* One time he forgot his cello in a taxi. Ma has recorded over 45 albums, and he has won many awards. These days, Yo-Yo Ma performs with a group called the "Silk Road Ensemble." The group has musicians from many countries and many cultures. They perform all over the world. Yo-Yo Ma is truly an international musician.

Paragraph

DESCRIBING A PLACE

Write a paragraph about one of the topics listed below (or the topic your teacher assigns). You will have 50 minutes.

Presentation

Model Paragraph

My Backyard

My backyard is a quiet and comfortable place to relax. On one side of the yard there is a covered patio with outdoor furniture. I love to sit and read there. Also, I like to eat there in nice weather. In the center of the yard there is a green lawn. It's fun to sit on the grass with friends on summer days. My backyard also has many beautiful plants. For example, there are fruit trees and many colorful flowers. The trees give shade on hot days. My backyard is beautiful, comfortable, and quiet. For these reasons, it is my favorite place to rest and relax.

Describing a Place

When you describe a place, you tell what it looks like and where things are in it. You can use the following language to describe a place:

There is / There are

In my classroom, there is a world map on the wall.

Prepositions of location

Canada is **in** North America.

There's a fountain **in the middle of** the park.

Descriptive adjectives

an **old** oak tree

a **peaceful** town

A paragraph describing a place should have these parts:

The topic sentence: The topic sentence should name the place you are going to describe. Then it should make a general statement about the place. For example: "My backyard is a quiet and comfortable place to relax."

Supporting sentences: These sentences provide details about the place. The sentences can answer questions like these:

What does the place look like?

What special things are in that place?

What can you do there?

How do you feel when you are there?

The conclusion: This sentence (or sentences) can repeat the main idea in your topic sentence. It can also add a final comment. For example: "My backyard is beautiful, comfortable, and quiet. For these reasons it is my favorite place to rest and relax."

1 Describe your house or apartment.

2 Describe your room.

3 Describe your neighborhood.

4 Describe your city.

Editing Checklist

Are the grammar, sentence structure, mechanics, and punctuation correct?

Is the vocabulary appropriate? Are the words spelled correctly?

Is the paragraph well organized, well developed, and clear?

DESCRIBING AN EVENT IN THE PAST

Model Paragraph

Last Friday with My Friend

Last Friday night, I went folk dancing with my roommate. It was my first time. We arrived at 7 o'clock. There were 40 or 50 people there. From 7 to 8 p.m., the teacher taught easy dances from Greece, Israel, Bulgaria, and Canada. At first, I was very confused. It was hard for me to remember the steps. But after a while, it got easier, and I started to enjoy myself. The other dancers helped me, too. At 8:30 there was an intermediate lesson. I was tired, so I watched the lesson and listened to the music. I had a really good time. I think folk dancing can be a great new hobby for me. It's good exercise, and I can meet a lot of nice people. I plan to go again next week.

Write a paragraph about one of the topics listed below (or the topic your teacher assigns). You will have 50 minutes.

Describing an Event in the Past

A paragraph that describes an event in the past often includes these parts:

The topic sentence: There are many ways to write a topic sentence about an event in the past. You can say what the event was and when it happened. You can also say what kind of event it was or how you felt about it. For example:

June 15, 2008, was a special day for me. On that day I graduated from college.

I had an interesting experience last weekend.

I will never forget my family's trip to Italy last summer.

I will never forget the first time I rode a horse.

Supporting sentences: Give details about the event. Tell what happened, what you remember, and how you felt. Use the simple past tense. To connect sentences and ideas, use past-time expressions, prepositional phrases, and time clauses. For example:

On that day, I woke up very early.

After the concert, we went for a walk on the beach.

When I opened the door, I saw a room full of people.

I hugged my parents one more time. Then I got on the train.

A concluding sentence: Repeat the main idea in different words or make a final comment about the event. For example, you can say what you remember or how you felt.

1 Tell about a happy event from your childhood.

2 Tell about what you did last weekend.

3 Tell about a vacation or trip you took in the past.

Editing Checklist

Are the grammar, sentence structure, mechanics, and punctuation correct?

Is the vocabulary appropriate? Are the words spelled correctly?

Is the paragraph well organized, well developed, and clear?

DESCRIBING FUTURE PLANS

Model Paragraph 1

My Future Plans

I want to accomplish three things after I finish school. First and most important, I want to get a job. My major is journalism. I want to get a job at a newspaper or at a radio station in my country, Peru. After I get a job, I want to get my own apartment. I love my family, but I want to be independent. I also plan to buy a car. My third goal is to learn Portuguese. Then I can work in Brazil. I think it is a very interesting country. I hope I can accomplish all these goals in the next two or three years.

Model Paragraph 2

Next Weekend

Next weekend is going to be a lot of fun. On Friday night, I am going to have dinner with my fiancé and his family. They are great people. I always laugh and have a good time with them. On Saturday, my fiancé and I are going to sail to Catalina Island with our friends Melinda and Jason. They have a sailboat. We are going to have a picnic on the island, and then we will sail back in the evening. On Saturday night, we will be tired, so we are going to stay home. Then on Sunday, I am going to have brunch with my best friend, Elsa. It is her birthday. Some other friends are going to meet us at the restaurant and surprise her. I know she's going to be very happy. I am looking forward to the weekend. It's going to be busy and a lot of fun.

Write a paragraph about one of the topics listed below (or the topic your teacher assigns). You will have 50 minutes.

Describing Future Plans

A paragraph that describes future plans often includes these parts:

The topic sentence: The topic sentence should state the event or events you are planning. You can also say how you feel about the future event. For example:

I am looking forward to (my college graduation).

I have big plans for (my summer vacation).

I plan to accomplish four things this weekend.

I am very excited about (my sister's wedding) this weekend.

Next weekend is going to be a lot of fun.

Supporting sentences: Organize the details of your paragraph by time order or listing order. To connect your ideas, you can use

time and listing words (first, second, later, finally)

time phrases (to begin, after that, in the end)

time clauses (after I graduate, before I buy my ticket)

A concluding sentence: Repeat the main idea in different words or make a final comment about your plans

1 Describe your plans for next weekend.

2 Describe your plans after you finish school.

3 Describe your next vacation plans.

Editing Checklist

Are the grammar, sentence structure, mechanics, and punctuation correct?

Is the vocabulary appropriate? Are the words spelled correctly?

Is the paragraph well organized, well developed, and clear?

_____

_____

_____

_____

_____

_____

_____

_____

_____

_____

_____

_____

_____

_____

_____

_____

_____

_____

DESCRIBING ROUTINES OR DAILY ACTIVITIES

Model Paragraph

Paul Nessen

Paul Nessen is a pre-school teacher. His pupils are four years old. Mr. Nessen's morning routine is always the same. At 8:00 a.m. the children arrive. He greets each child. Sometimes he takes a moment to talk to the parents. After all the children arrive, they sit down on the rug, and Mr. Nessen sings a "morning song" with them. Then they review the day of the week, the date, and the weather. After that, the class works on the "unit of the week," for example, colors, animals, jobs, or food. The children talk, listen, read, draw, play games, and do other activities related to the unit. At 9:45, the children go outside for recess, and Mr. Nessen takes a break. When the children come back, they continue learning about the unit of the week. At 11:15, Mr. Nessen announces that it's time to clean up. The children put away their materials. Then they sit on the rug again, and the class talks or sings a "good-bye" song. At 11:45, the parents arrive, and Mr. Nessen says good-bye to the children. School is finished for the day.

Write a paragraph about one of the topics listed below (or the topic your teacher assigns). You will have 50 minutes.

Describing Routines or Daily Activities

A paragraph that describes a daily routine should include these parts:

The topic sentence: The topic sentence should name the subject of the paragraph and use words to show that the paragraph is about someone's routine or daily activities. For example:

I have the same routine every weekday morning.

Saturday is a relaxing day for Sonia.

Tony Hernandez is a truck driver for a paper company. He has the same schedule every week.

Supporting sentences: Describe the routine or activities in time order. Use simple present tense. To connect sentences and ideas, use time clauses, time-order words and phrases, frequency adverbs, and prepositional phrases of time. For example:

Dr. Gelberg usually gets up at 6:00 a.m.

Mark walks his dog before he leaves for work.

First, I have a cup of coffee. Then I take a shower.

When the bell rings, the children go to their classrooms.

A concluding sentence: Repeat the main idea in different words, make a final comment about the routine, or simply end the paragraph with the last part of the routine.

1 Describe your typical week.

2 Describe your typical weekend.

3 Describe someone else's typical week.

4 Describe your or someone else's typical day.

Editing Checklist

Are the grammar, sentence structure, mechanics, and punctuation correct?

Is the vocabulary appropriate? Are the words spelled correctly?

Is the paragraph well organized, well developed, and clear?

EXPRESSING AN OPINION

Model Paragraph

My Eating Habits

I think my eating habits are very healthy. For example, I only eat small meals, and I don't eat snacks between meals. This habit helps me stay thin. Next, I eat lots of fresh vegetables and fruit. They are full of vitamins and minerals, and they keep me healthy. I only eat a little meat, eggs, and cheese, because they have a lot of cholesterol. Instead of meat, I get protein from beans or tofu. Finally, I drink a cup of coffee every day, and for dessert I like to eat a little bit of dark chocolate. Coffee and chocolate are good for your heart, and they taste great! I hope my good eating habits will help me live a long life.

Write a paragraph about one of the topics listed below (or the topic your teacher assigns). You will have 50 minutes.

Expressing an Opinion

A paragraph that expresses an opinion should include these parts:

A topic sentence: State your topic and give your opinion about it. Use expressions for stating an opinion. For example:

I think my eating habits are very healthy.

In my opinion, it is very important to learn a second language.

Nowadays, most people spend too much time using electronic devices.

Supporting sentences: Support your opinion with reasons or examples. For example:

One reason is that learning a second language makes you smarter.

For example, I do not eat between meals.

For example, they check their phone for messages every five minutes.

A concluding sentence: Your concluding sentence can summarize the reasons for your opinion, state your hope for the future, or state your final opinion. For example:

I hope my good eating habits will help me live a long life.

For all these reasons, I think it is a good idea to learn more than one language.

In conclusion, put down your phone, go outside, and take a walk!

Express your opinion on one of the following topics:

1 Is it important to learn more than one language?

2 In general, do you have good or bad work habits?

3 Do people spend too much time on electronic devices?

Editing Checklist

Are the grammar, sentence structure, mechanics, and punctuation correct?

Is the vocabulary appropriate? Are the words spelled correctly?

Is the paragraph well organized, well developed, and clear?

GIVING ADVICE

Model Paragraph

How to Stay Healthy for Life

Do you want to stay healthy for your whole life? Then follow my advice. First, eat properly. Eat lots of fruit and vegetables. Don't eat sugar, fatty foods, or processed foods. And most important: Don't eat too much. Try to stay thin. Next, get lots of exercise. Run, swim, clean your house, or work in your garden. Move your body! Try to exercise at least three or four hours every week. My third suggestion is to get lots of sleep. When you sleep, your body repairs itself. Sleep reduces stress and gives you energy. It is very important. In my opinion, these are the best ways to stay healthy.

Write a paragraph about one of the topics listed below (or the topic your teacher assigns). You will have 50 minutes.

Giving Advice

A paragraph that gives advice should include these parts:

A topic sentence: Use words like "advice," "suggestions", "rules", "steps" or "ways" to state your topic. For example:

Here are some useful ways to improve your English.

If you want to stay healthy, follow my advice.

I have three suggestions for finding a good wife.

Follow these steps to grow delicious tomatoes.

Supporting sentences: List your suggestions using connecting words like first, second, next, and finally. Use the imperative form of the verb. For example:

First, ask your friends and relatives to help you.

Make sure to sleep eight hours every night.

Finally, keep a vocabulary notebook.

A concluding sentence: Repeat your main idea in different words, summarize the suggestions, or say what will happen if the reader follows your advice. For example:

If you follow my advice, your English will improve very quickly.

1 What are the best ways to improve your English?

2 What are the best ways to stay healthy?

3 What are the best ways to find a good husband or wife?

Editing Checklist

Are the grammar, sentence structure, mechanics, and punctuation correct?

Is the vocabulary appropriate? Are the words spelled correctly?

Is the paragraph well organized, well developed, and clear?

_____

_____

_____

_____

_____

_____

_____

_____

_____

_____

_____

_____

_____

_____

_____

_____

_____

_____

_____

_____

_____

_____

_____

_____

_____

INTRODUCING PEOPLE

Model Paragraph 1

All About Me

I would like to introduce myself. My name is Yousuf Selim, and I am from Jordan. I am 24 years old. I am studying engineering at Emory University in Atlanta, Georgia. I am married, and my wife is here in Atlanta with me. I have an interesting hobby. I like to watch birds. On weekends, my wife and I like to go hiking. We are enjoying our life in the United States.

Model Paragraph 2

My Cousin Michelle

It is my pleasure to introduce you to my cousin Michelle. She was born in the United States. She is 32 years old, and she lives in New York City. Michelle has an interesting job. She is a graphic designer for an advertising company. I love spending time with Michelle. She tells funny jokes. She is a lot of fun.

Write a paragraph about one of the topics listed below (or the topic your teacher assigns). You will have 50 minutes.

Introducing People

A paragraph introducing a person should include these parts:

A topic sentence: Give the name or identity of the person you are introducing. For example:

I would like to introduce myself.

Psy is a famous entertainer in my country, South Korea.

It is my pleasure to introduce you to my Aunt Michelle.

This is a photo of my boss, Mr. Terry Bak.

Supporting sentences: Write several sentences to introduce the person. For example, you can give the answers to these questions:

What is your relationship to this person?

Where is this person from?

How old is he or she?

What languages does he or she speak?

Is this person married? Does he or she have children?

Where does the person live?

What does the person do?

What is the person studying?

What does he or she like to do on weekends?

A concluding sentence: Say how you feel about this person. If you are writing about yourself, write a final sentence about your life. You can also write about your future plans.

1 Choose a photo. Imagine you know this person. Describe the person.

2 Introduce a person in your family.

3 Introduce a famous person.

4 Introduce yourself.

Editing Checklist

Are the grammar, sentence structure, mechanics, and punctuation correct?

Is the vocabulary appropriate? Are the words spelled correctly?

Is the paragraph well organized, well developed, and clear?

_____

_____

_____

_____

_____

_____

_____

_____

_____

_____

_____

_____

_____

_____

_____

_____

_____

_____

_____

_____

WRITING INSTRUCTIONS

> **Presentation**
>
> Model Paragraph
>
> **How to Clean a Kitchen Floor**
>
> I am very good at cleaning my kitchen floor. Here is how I do it. There are three steps: Sweep, wash, and polish. First, I sweep the floor. Then I am ready to wash it. I fill a bucket with water and add one capful of floor cleaner. I put my mop in the bucket of water, get it wet, and wring it out. Then I clean a small section of the floor. I repeat this step until the whole floor is clean. Then I wait about 15 minutes until the floor is dry. Finally, I use the mop to polish the floor with liquid floor polish. Then I wait I another 30 minutes. The result is a clean, shiny floor that looks really great!

Write a paragraph about one of the topics listed below (or the topic your teacher assigns). You will have 50 minutes.

Giving Instructions

Paragraphs that give instructions are sometimes called "how-to" paragraphs because they explain how to do or make something.

A paragraph that gives instructions should include these parts:

The topic sentence: The topic sentence should name the topic and say that the paragraph will give instructions about it. For example:

To make a delicious bean dip for chips, follow these easy steps.

It is very easy to order take-out pizza online.

Here is a simple way to wash a dog.

Supporting sentences: Divide the instructions into a list of steps or suggestions. Name each one. Then explain each of them in one or two sentences. Introduce each new step with transitions such as *first, second, then, next, finally*.

Use the command form of verbs to give instructions. For example:

- Fill a pot with cold water.
- Don't walk on the floor until it is dry.

A concluding sentence: Repeat the main idea in different words, or say what will happen if the reader follows your instructions.

1 Describe how to cook your favorite dish.

2 Describe how to do something that you are very good at doing.

3 Describe how to register for English classes.

Editing Checklist

Are the grammar, sentence structure, mechanics, and punctuation correct?

Is the vocabulary appropriate? Are the words spelled correctly?

Is the paragraph well organized, well developed, and clear?

Special Writing Skills

WRITING LETTERS AND POSTCARDS

Presentation

Model Paragraph 1

March 22, 2014

Dear Aunt Beth,

How are you? Mom says you had a bad cold last week. I hope you're feeling better. I am writing to invite you to attend my college graduation ceremony. It will take place on June 18, 2014. I know it's only March now, but I want to give you time to find a cheap airline ticket. It's going to be a very exciting weekend. I really hope you can come!

Love,

Mary Ellen

Model Paragraph 2

June 29, 2014

Dear Mom and Dad,

Prague is an amazing city! Yesterday we visited Prague Castle and went to a concert in the evening. Today we walked across the Charles Bridge. We're going to the Jewish Museum next. Our guesthouse is great, and the food is fantastic. Everything is perfect! I miss you!

Love,

Lina

Mr. and Mrs. Simon Ellis

39 Spruce Lane

Allentown, Pennsylvania 18103

Write a paragraph about one of the topics listed below (or the topic your teacher assigns). You will have 50 minutes.

Write a friendly letter or postcard

A friendly letter or postcard should have these parts:

Heading: If you want to include your address, write it in the upper right corner. Write the date under it. However, in most letters you do not need to write your address.

Greeting: Common greetings are:

Dear _____ ,

Hi _____ ,

Hello _____ ,

Write a comma after the person's name.

Body: This is where your text goes.

Closing: End your letter politely. Some common closings are:

Love,

Your friend,

Take care,

Write a comma after the closing.

Signature: Write your name under the closing.

A postcard is similar to a letter, but the message is very short.

Write the message on the left side of the postcard. Write the recipient's address on the right side.

1 Write a letter inviting a friend to an event.

2 Write a postcard to a family member describing your experiences during a trip.

Editing Checklist

Are the grammar, sentence structure, mechanics, and punctuation correct?

Is the vocabulary appropriate? Are the words spelled correctly?

Is the letter well organized, well developed, and clear?

_____

_____

_____

_____

_____

_____

_____

_____

_____

_____

WRITING EMAILS

Model Paragraph 1

Hey Allen,

Some guys are coming over to watch the football game Saturday afternoon around 3. Can you come? Let me know so I can buy enough food.

See ya,

Max

Model Paragraph 2

Dear Lexie,

I want to confirm my plans to visit you and Pete two weeks from now. I'm arriving Friday at 11:00 a.m. on Delta flight 3320 from Atlanta. I'll call you as soon as the plane lands. If you can pick me up, great. If not, I'll take a cab to your house.

I can't wait to see you guys. I hope the weather is good!

Love & see you soon,

Amy

Write a paragraph about one of the topics listed below (or the topic your teacher assigns). You will have 50 minutes.

Writing Emails

A friendly email should include these parts:

Heading:

To: This is the email address of the person who will receive the email.

Cc: Type in the addresses of people who will receive a copy of your email.

Subject: This states the topic of your email or the reason you are writing. It is like the title of a paragraph. It is usually short.

Greeting: Email greetings are usually short and informal. For example:

Hey Sandra,

Hi Tom,

Alex –

Body: This is where your message goes. It is usually short. It is fine to use contractions and abbreviations.

Closing: Closings for informal emails are optional. For example:

Talk to you later,

See ya,

Take care,

Bye,

Love,

Signature: Type your name at the end of your message.

1 Write an email inviting a friend to a party at your home.

2 Write an email message to a friend about your plans to visit him or her.

Editing Checklist

Are the grammar, sentence structure, mechanics, and punctuation correct?

Is the vocabulary appropriate? Are the words spelled correctly?

Is the letter well organized, well developed, and clear?

_____

_____

_____

_____

_____

_____

_____

_____

_____

_____

_____

_____

_____

_____

_____

_____

_____

Appendix 1
Common Irregular Verbs

Base Form	Simple Past	Base Form	Simple Past
be	was, were	keep	kept
become	became	know	knew
begin	began	leave	left
bite	bit	lose	lost
blow	blew	make	made
break	broke	meet	met
bring	brought	pay	paid
build	built	put	put
buy	bought	read	read
catch	caught	run	ran
choose	chose	say	said
come	came	see	saw
cost	cost	sell	sold
cut	cut	send	sent
do	did	sing	sang
drink	drank	sit	sat
drive	drove	sleep	slept
eat	ate	speak	spoke
fall	fell	spend	spent
feel	felt	stand	stood
find	found	steal	stole
fly	flew	swim	swam
forget	forgot	take	took
get	got	teach	taught
give	gave	tell	told
go	went	think	thought
grow	grew	throw	threw
have	had	understand	understood
hear	heard	wake up	woke up
hold	held	wear	wore
hurt	hurt	write	wrote

Appendix 2
Transition Signals for Order of Importance

When you list your ideas in order of importance, you list them from least important to most important or most important to least important.

Transition Signals	Examples
first, first of all	**First**, the hotel is in a noisy area.
second(ly), next, also, in addition	**Also**, the service at the hotel is poor.
most important(ly), most of all, finally	**Most importantly**, the rooms at the hotel are hot and dirty.

Appendix 3
Transition Signals for Time Order

Use time-order transitions to show the order of events in a narrative or steps in a process.

Time-Order Words	Examples
first, second, third	*(Narrative)*
to begin, to start	**First**, Mr. Kana drinks his coffee. **Next**, he takes a shower.
next, then, after that, later	*(Process)*
finally, last	**To begin**, pour water into the coffee maker. **After that**, measure the coffee. **Finally**, pour a little milk into the black coffee.

Appendix 4
Transition Signals for Giving Examples

Transitions	Examples
for example	My brother is a neat person. **For example**, he keeps his desk very clean.
for instance	Linda is interested in Latin American dance. **For instance**, she is learning the rumba.

Appendix 5
Common Spelling Errors

Words	Rules	Examples
accept, except	*Accept* is a verb. It means to take something that someone offers you.	He **accepted** the job.
	Except is a preposition. It is used to show things or people that are not included in a statement.	Everybody came to the party **except** Ellen.
for, four	*For* is a preposition. It has many meanings. For example, it means "meant to be used" or "given to someone or something."	Here is a letter **for** you.
	Four is a number.	I have **four** sisters.
its, it's	*Its* is a possessive adjective. It means "belonging to something."	The tree lost all **its** leaves.
	It's is a contraction. It means "it is."	**It's** a nice day. Let's go to the beach.
loose, lose	*Loose* is an adjective. It means something is not tight.	These pants are **loose** on me.
	Lose is a verb. It means to not have something anymore or not to know where it is.	Don't **lose** my cell phone.
right, write	*Right* is an adjective. It means "correct."	Your answer is **right**.
	Write is a verb. It means to communicate with a pencil, pen, or computer.	I need to **write** a paper for my history class.
their, there, they're	*Their* is a possessive adjective. It means "belonging to them."	Where is **their** house?
	There is an adverb. It means in or near a place.	Please put the books **there**.
	They're is a contraction. It means "they are."	**They're** tired.
to, too, two	*To* is a preposition. It has many meanings. For example, it means "in the direction of."	We drove **to** the store.
	Too is an adverb. It means "also."	Joe has blond hair, and his sister does, **too**.
	Two is a number.	The family owns **two** cars.
you're, your	*You're* is a contraction. It means "you are."	**You're** late.
	Your is a possessive adjective. It means something belongs to you.	Is that **your** dog?

Appendix 6
Subordinating Conjunctions

Subordinating conjunctions are words that introduce dependent clauses. The following are common types of subordinating conjunctions.

To introduce time clauses

Conjunctions	Examples
after	We washed the dishes **after** we ate.
before	**Before** you can get a driver's license, you have to take a test.
when	**When** Ella finishes college, she plans to travel.

To introduce clauses of reason

Conjunctions	Example
because	Jack was late to work **because** his car had a flat tire.

To introduce conditions

Conjunctions	Example
if	**If** I don't eat breakfast, then I get very hungry around 9 a.m.

Appendix 7

Coordinating Conjunctions

The coordinating conjunctions are *and*, *or*, *but*, and *so*. Use them to connect words, phrases, or clauses.

Conjunctions	Example
and	I like sandwiches with peanut butter **and** jelly.
	Mary washed the dishes, **and** John cleaned the floor.
or	You can go downtown by bus **or** by subway.
	This weekend we'll stay home, **or** we'll go to Miami.
but	Eric is very tall **but** very thin.
	Karen has a new phone, **but** she doesn't know how to use it.
so	Abby's flight to Chicago was late, **so** she missed her connecting flight to Toronto.

Appendix 8

Subject, Object, and Possessive Pronouns and Possessive Adjectives

Forms	Singular	Plural
Subject pronouns	I, you, he, she, it	we, you, they
Object pronouns	me, you, him, her, it	us, you, them
Possessive pronouns	mine, yours, his, hers, its	ours, yours, theirs
Possessive adjectives	my, your, his, her, its	our, your, their

Appendix 9
Prepositions of Time and Place

Prepositions of Time		Examples
Use *in* with	parts of the day	in the morning, in the evening
	months	in December
	years	in 1975
	seasons	in the summer
Use *on* with	days of the week	on Tuesday
	specific dates	on November 13th
	holidays	on Thanksgiving
	special days	on my birthday
Use *at* with	specific times	at 3 o'clock, at 6 p.m.
Use *from . . . to* with	a span of time	from 2 to 4 a.m., from Monday to Friday, from January to June

Prepositions of Place	Examples
above	There's a clock **above** the bookcase.
across from	There is a sofa **across from** the desk.
beside, next to	There's a lamp **beside / next to** the computer table.
between	There's a sofa **between** the file cabinets.
in front of	There's a tree **in front of** the house.
in the middle of	There's a TV **in the middle of** the room.
in, inside	There is food **in / inside** the refrigerator.
on	There are lots of papers **on** the desk.
on both sides of	There are file cabinets **on both sides of** the sofa.
on the (your) right, on the (your) left	When you enter the room, the closet is **on the right**. There's a bookcase **on the left**.
on top of	There's a computer **on top of** the computer table.
outside	There is a hallway **outside** the office.
over	There are windows **over** the sofa.
under	There are power cords **under** the computer table.

Appendix 10
Common Noncount Nouns

advice	history	pepper
biology	homework	rain
bread	ice	rice
butter	ice cream	salt
cheese	information	sand
coffee	jewelry	snow
corn	juice	soup
crime	love	spaghetti
fish	luck	sugar
food	mail	tea
fruit	meat	time
furniture	milk	traffic
garbage	money	vocabulary
geography	music	water
happiness	noise	weather
help	oil	work
	paper	

Appendix 11
Spelling of Plural Count Nouns

Rules	Singular	Plural
Add -s to form the plural of most count nouns.	pencil	pencils
	cat	cats
Add -es to form the plural of nouns that end in a consonant + o.	tomato	tomatoes
Add -es to form the plural of nouns that end in *ch, sh, x,* or *ss.*	kiss	kisses
	box	boxes
	witch	witches
	wish	wishes
To form the plural of words that end in consonant + *y*, change the *y* to *i* and add -es.	party	parties
To form the plural of words that end in vowel + *y*, add -s.	boy	boys
Some nouns do not have a singular form		clothes
		pants
Some plural nouns have an irregular plural form.	child	children
	foot	feet
	man	men
	person	people
	tooth	teeth
	woman	women

Appendix 12

Spelling of Third-Person Singular Present Verbs

Rules	Base Form	Third Person
Add -*s* to form the third-person singular of most present singular verbs.	brag	brags
Add -*es* to verbs ending in *s, z, x, sh,* and *ch*.	kiss	kisses
	buzz	buzzes
	fix	fixes
	push	pushes
	watch	watches
If a verb ends in consonant + -*y*, change the *y* to *i* and add -*es*.	try	tries
If a verb ends in vowel + -*y*, do not change the ending.	pay	pays
Have, be, and *do* have irregular third-person singular forms.	be	is
	do	does
	have	has

Appendix 13

Spelling of Present Participles

Rules	Base Form	Present Participle
Add -*ing* to the base form of most verbs.	walk	walking
If a verb ends in -e, drop the e and add -*ing*.	come	coming
If a one-syllable verb ends in consonant + vowel + consonant (CVC), then double the last consonant and add -ing.	sit	sitting
Do not double the last consonant if a word ends in *w, x,* or *y.*	flow	flowing
	fix	fixing
	play	playing
In words of more than one syllable that end in consonant + vowel + consonant (CVC), double the last consonant if the syllable is stressed.	permit	permitting

Appendix 14
Spelling of Regular Past-tense Verbs

Rules	Base Form	Past Tense
If a verb ends in a consonant, add -ed.	jump	jumped
If a verb ends in -e, add -d.	like	liked
If a verb ends in consonant + -y, then change the y to i and add -ed.	carry	carried
If the verb ends in vowel + -y, then do not change the y to i. Just add -ed.	play	played
If a one-syllable verb ends in consonant + vowel + consonant (CVC), then double the last consonant and add -ed.	jog	jogged
Do not double the last consonant if a word ends in w, x, or y. Just add -ed.	fix	fixed
In words of more than one syllable that end in consonant + vowel + consonant (CVC), double the last consonant and add -ed.	permit	permitted

Post-Test 1

In Post-Test 1, you will demonstrate how well you understand sentence structure, grammar, punctuation, mechanics, and organization. You have 50 minutes to complete the test. To mark your answer, circle the letter of the correct choice.

1 My city doesn't have _____ airport.

   a a

   b an

   c some

   d the

2 Last year it snowed ___ October.

   a on

   b at

   c in

   d to

3 Disneyworld is ___ Orlando, Florida.

   a by

   b at

   c on

   d in

4 I can't go out tonight because I have _____ .

   a a homework

   b an homework

   c homeworks

   d homework

5 The music at the concert _____ very loud.

   a are

   b was

   c were

   d am

6 After college I _____ to Chicago.

   a move

   b will moving

   c am going to move

   d moving

7 I'm tired. I don't want to go to school _____ morning.

   a in

   b next

   c this

   d on

8 The flowers _____ beautiful.

   a be

   b am

   c is

   d are

9 The child _____ to eat vegetables.

   a not like

   b no like

   c doesn't like

   d never like

10 Mr. Evans never _____ a hat.

   a is wearing

   b are wearing

   c wears

   d will wear

11 Mary _____ in New York last week.

   a be

   b was

   c were

   d am

12 My roommate and I _____ dinner together last night.

   a cooked

   b cooking

   c cook

   d cooks

13 Tom _____ his car last week.

   a sell

   b sold

   c selling

   d selled

14 There _____ two paintings on the wall.

   a be

   b was

   c are

   d is

15 _____ milk in the refrigerator.

   a No is

   b There is no

   c Is no

   d There no

16 Where are Carol and Sam? _____ late.

   a Theyr'e

   b The'yre

   c They're

   d Th'eyre

17 I like my _____ family. He has really nice parents and siblings.

   a roommates

   b roommate

   c roommates'

   d roommate's

18 Circle the letter of the correct sentence.

   a when do you want to leave

   b when do you want to leave?

   c When do you want to leave

   d When do you want to leave?

19 Circle the letter of the sentence with correct capitalization.

   a We always spend christmas in florida.

   b We always spend Christmas in florida.

   c We always spend christmas in florida.

   d We always spend Christmas in Florida.

20 Circle the letter of the sentence with correct punctuation.

   a I liked the book, because it was funny.

   b I liked the book because, it was funny.

   c I liked the book because it was funny.

   d I liked, the book because it was funny.

21 Circle the letter of the sentence with correct punctuation.

   a Donna is a vegetarian so she never eats meat.

   b Donna is a vegetarian so, she never eats meat.

   c Donna is a vegetarian, so she never eats meat.

   d Donna is a vegetarian so she, never eats meat.

22 Circle the letter of the sentence with correct punctuation.

   a On Christmas morning the children woke up very early.

   b On Christmas morning the children, woke up very early.

   c On Christmas morning the children woke up, very early.

   d On Christmas morning, the children woke up very early.

23 It snowed on Tuesday, _____ it rained on Wednesday.

   a and

   b or

   c if

   d so

24 Shira exercises every day, _____ she doesn't enjoy it.

   a so

   b or

   c but

   d if

25 The shoes are expensive, _____ they are not comfortable.

   a but

   b if

   c or

   d so

26 John will wear his old suit, _____ he will buy a new one.

   a and

   b but

   c or

   d so

27 Ron quit his job, _____ he has a lot of free time.

   a then

   b so

   c but

   d or

28 Circle the letter of the correct sentence.

   a If the weather is nice, we will go to the beach tomorrow.

   b If the weather nice, we go to the beach tomorrow.

   c If the weather will be nice, we go to the beach tomorrow.

   d If the weather is nice, we go to the beach tomorrow.

29 Circle the letter of the correct sentence.

   a I run, when my foot hurts.

   b When I run my foot hurts.

   c My foot hurts, when I run.

   d When I run, my foot hurts.

30 Circle the letter of the correct sentence.

   a I opened the window. Because the room was hot.

   b I opened the window, because the room was hot.

   c I opened the window, because, the room was hot.

   d I opened the window because the room was hot.

31 Circle the letter of the correct sentence.

    a After they retired, my grandparents moved to Costa Rica.

    b My grandparents retired, after they moved to Costa Rica.

    c After they retired my grandparents moved to Costa Rica.

    d My grandparents retired. After, they moved to Costa Rica.

32 Circle the letter of the correct sentence.

    a Before I left the office, I turned off the computer.

    b Before, I left the office, I turned off the computer.

    c I left the office, before I turned off the computer.

    d I left the office. Before I turned off the computer.

33 Circle the letter of the correct sentence.

    a I will walk the dog, I will go to work.

    b I will walk the dog, then I will go to work.

    c I will walk the dog then I will go to work.

    d I will walk the dog. Then I will go to work.

34 The apples in the refrigerator _____ delicious.

    a am

    b are

    c be

    d is

35 It is easy to make spaghetti. First of all, boil two quarts of water. _____ , put half a package of dry spaghetti in the water.

    a After

    b After that

    c Next of all

    d Another

36 Exercising every day helps me in three ways. First, it helps me stay thin. _____ , it gives me energy. Third, it helps me sleep well.

    a In addition

    b For that reason

    c For example

    d Finally

37 Read the paragraph. Circle the letter of the sentence that does not belong.

1) Connie is a very athletic person. 2) She loves to play all kinds of sports. 3) She belongs to a tennis club where she can play with other people. 4) She also likes to run and swim at the beach. 5) In addition, she takes two dance classes every week. 6) Connie works at a coffee shop. 7) Connie is very busy with all her sports and athletic activities.

    a Sentence 1

    b Sentence 3

    c Sentence 5

    d Sentence 6

38 I like driving a large car for three reasons. One reason is that large cars are safer than small cars. If I have an accident, it is better to be in a large, heavy car. _____ is that large cars are more comfortable. I am tall. In a small car my head hits the ceiling, but in a large car I have plenty of room.

a Because

b For example

c Another reason

d Also

39 The ancient Chinese invented many useful things. _____ , they invented paper, silk, and noodles.

a In addition

b The most important

c At first

d For example

40 Read the topic sentence for a paragraph. Which words tell you what the paragraph will discuss? Circle the letter of the correct answer.

Topic Sentence: You should follow four steps when you write an essay for your English class.

a should follow

b four steps

c write an essay

d your English class

Post-Test 2

In Post-Test 2, you will demonstrate how well you can write about a topic. Pay attention to sentence structure, grammar, punctuation, mechanics, organization, and vocabulary. Write about the following topic or the topic your teacher assigns. You have 50 minutes to complete the test.

Write a paragraph about your progress in studying English. How difficult was it when you first started studying English? What improvements do you see now? What are you going to do to improve your English in the future?

_____

_____

_____

_____

_____

_____

_____

_____

_____

_____

_____

_____

_____

_____

_____

_____

_____

_____

_____

_____

ANSWER KEY

PRE-TEST

Pre-Test 1 pp. 1–6

1. c, 2. c, 3. b, 4. a, 5. a, 6. b, 7. c, 8. a,
9. b, 10. a, 11. a, 12. d, 13. c, 14. c, 15. c,
16. b, 17. b, 18. d, 19. c, 20. b, 21. a,
22. c, 23. d, 24. b, 25. d, 26. a, 27. d,
28. a, 29. d, 30. c, 31. b, 32. d, 33. c,
34. b, 35. b, 36. c, 37. c, 38. c, 39. b, 40. c

Pre-Test 2 p. 7

Answers will vary.

PUNCTUATION AND MECHANICS

Apostrophes

CONTRACTIONS WITH AUXILIARY *BE* AND *DO*

Practice 1 p. 9

1. It's
2. She's
3. aren't
4. We're
5. doesn't
6. I'm
7. it's
8. don't
9. They're
10. You're
11. isn't

Practice 2 p. 9

1. Im, were
2. dont
3. isnt, Theyre
4. arent
5. doesnt
6. Hes

POSSESSIVES

Practice 1 p. 10

1. mother's
2. Linda's
3. man's
4. men's
5. neighbors'
6. roommate's
7. dogs'
8. child's

9. children's
10. teacher's
11. teachers'

Practice 2 p. 11

1. girls'
2. professors'
3. Smiths'
4. grandparents
5. students'
6. boys'
7. wives
8. brothers'
9. dogs'
10. desks
11. questions

Capital Letters

BEGINNING A SENTENCE

Practice 1 p. 12

<u>my</u> name is Anush. I am from Armenia.
<u>my</u> first language is Armenian. <u>i</u> also speak
Russian. Now I live in Los Angeles, California.
<u>the</u> city has a large Armenian population.
<u>today</u> is the first day of my new English
class. I want to speak English well. <u>it</u> is very
important for my future. When I finish school,
I want to be a veterinarian. <u>it's</u> going to take a
long time, but I don't mind. I love animals. <u>my</u>
friends say I'm going to be a good vet.

Practice 2 pp. 12–13

1. My cousin drives a red sports car.
2. I like to drink coffee.
3. The movie starts at 8:00.
4. That's a very sad story.
5. John usually studies in the library.
6. Are you from Australia?
7. In my family, my father usually cooks dinner.
8. The price of stamps is going up.
9. What do you like to do in your free time?

PROPER NOUNS

Practice 1 p. 14

1. dr
2. adrienne
3. marseille
4. france

5. europe
9. states
6. tuesday
10. veterans
7. november
11. day
8. united

Practice 2 p. 14

1. My birthday is January 18th.
2. I can meet you on Thursday at 6.
3. When is your appointment with Dr. Jackson?
4. My father's office is on Orange Avenue.
5. Yolanda is studying Chinese.
6. The state of Alaska has a lot of oil.
7. My family moved to Cleveland, Ohio, on June 15, 2008.
8. The largest country in South America is Brazil.

PARAGRAPH TITLES

Practice 1 p. 15

1. b, 2. b, 3. b, 4. a, 5. a, 6. b, 7. b, 8. b

Practice 2 pp. 15–16

1. Around the World in Eighty Days
2. My Year in Cairo
3. A Serious Mistake
4. The Health Benefits of Chocolate
5. An Unusual Job
6. It's Never Too Late
7. A Perfect Pair of Boots
8. How to Make a Perfect Cup of Coffee
9. One World, Many Languages

Commas

COMPLEX SENTENCES WITH *AFTER, WHEN, BECAUSE, AND IF*

Practice 1 p. 17

1. b, 2. a, 3. b, 4. b, 5. b, 6. a, 7. b, 8. a, 9. b

Practice 2 pp. 17–18

1. a, 2. b, 3. b, 4. c, 5. a, 6. c, 7. a, 8. c, 9. b

COMPOUND SENTENCES WITH *AND, BUT, SO, AND OR*

Practice 1 pp. 18–19

1. b, 2. b, 3. a, 4. a, 5. a, 6. b, 7. b, 8. b

Practice 2 p. 19

1. tired, and I want to
2. years old, and my daughter
3. studied hard, but I failed
4. late, so I need
5. have lunch now, or I'll eat
6. the wrong color, so
7. was long, and it was hard
8. to the mall, but we didn't buy
9. wear a tuxedo, or he'll

PUNCTUATING DATES

Practice 1 p. 20

1. January 1, 2010
2. February 12, 1986
3. July 4, 1776
4. December 25, 1945
5. April 12, 2004
6. October 31, 1999
7. September 3, 1919
8. July 14, 1789

Practice 2 p. 21

1. b, 2. a, 3. b, 4. a, 5. b, 6. b, 7. a, 8. a, 9. a

ITEMS IN A SERIES

Practice 1 p. 22

1. a, 2. b, 3. a, 4. b, 5. b, 6. a, 7. a, 8. b

Practice 2 pp. 22–23

1. Prague, Vienna, and Budapest
2. trees, grass, and flowers
3. Monday, Tuesday, and Wednesday
4. grandparents, uncles, aunts, and cousins
5. tea, coffee, or juice

6. English, Spanish, French, German, Polish, and Italian
7. salty, sweet, or spicy
8. reading, swimming, and playing guitar
9. Mike, Sara, Thomas, or Ahmed

TIME SIGNALS

Practice 1 p. 24

1. b, 2. a, 3. a, 4. b, 5. a, 6. b, 7. a, 8. a, 9. b

Practice 2 p. 24

1. b, 2. b, 3. a, 4. a, 5. a, 6. b, 7. a, 8. b, 9. a

End Punctuation

Practice 1 p. 25

1. .	4. !	7. .	10. .
2. .	5. ?	8. ?	11. !
3. .	6. .	9. .	

Practice 2 p. 26

1. My name is Anush.
2. Do you like doughnuts?
3. Doughnuts are round cakes.
4. They have a hole in the middle.
5. Doughnuts are my favorite American food.
6. I think they are delicious!
7. Look at that big dog!
8. What kind of dog is it?
9. It is a Great Dane.
10. How much does it weigh?
11. Great Danes are very gentle.

Paragraph Format

Practice 1 p. 29

1. a, 2. b, 3. c, 4. b, 5. d

Practice 2 p. 30

1. b, 2. b, 3. a, 4. a, 5. b, 6. b, 7. b, 8. a, 9. b

Spelling

THIRD-PERSON SINGULAR -S

Practice 1 p. 32

1. b, 2. a, 3. b, 4. a, 5. a, 6. b, 7. a, 8. b, 9. a, 10. a, 11. a, 12. a

Practice 2 p. 32

1. speaks	7. goes
2. writes	8. reads
3. studies	9. brushes
4. pays	10. fixes
5. watches	11. passes
6. flies	

-ING

Practice 1 pp. 33–34

1. b, 2. a, 3. a, 4. a, 5. a, 6. b, 7. b, 8. a, 9. b, 10. a, 11. b

Practice 2 p. 34

1. speaking	7. going
2. writing	8. cutting
3. studying	9. smiling
4. clapping	10. raining
5. crying	11. passing
6. blowing	

REGULAR PAST-TENSE VERBS

Practice 1 pp. 35–36

1. a, 2. a, 3. b, 4. a, 5. a, 6. b, 7. a, 8. a, 9. a, 10. a, 11. a

Practice 2 p. 36

1. cleaned	7. taxed
2. watched	8. carried
3. studied	9. shaved
4. clapped	10. rained
5. cried	11. passed
6. allowed	

GRAMMAR

Articles

ARTICLES *A* AND *AN*

Practice 1 p. 38

1. a	5. X	9. a
2. an	6. X	10. an
3. an	7. an	
4. a	8. a	

Practice 2 p. 38

1. a	5. X	9. X
2. a	6. a	10. a
3. X	7. an	11. an
4. an	8. a	

A VS. *THE*

Practice 1 p. 39

1. an, a, The	3. the	5. The
2. the	4. a, the, the	6. an

Practice 2 pp. 40–41

1. a	4. the, The	7. the
2. the	5. a	8. the
3. the	6. the	9. the

Adjectives

ADJECTIVES WITH *BE*

Practice 1 p. 42

pretty, short, blond, blue, short, thin, special, cute, light, careful

Practice 2 pp. 42–43

1. Incorrect	7. Incorrect
2. Correct	8. Correct
3. Correct	9. Correct
4. Incorrect	10. Incorrect
5. Incorrect	11. Incorrect
6. Correct	

ADJECTIVE ORDER

Practice 1 pp. 44–45

1. Correct	7. Incorrect
2. Incorrect	8. Incorrect
3. Correct	9. Correct
4. Incorrect	10. Correct
5. Incorrect	11. Incorrect
6. Correct	

Practice 2 pp. 45–46

1. traditional Greek
2. beautiful white silk
3. long lace
4. large Greek
5. formal gray
6. many wonderful wedding
7. tall antique silver
8. six beautiful rose
9. square glass coffee
10. three small

POSSESSIVE ADJECTIVES

Practice 1 p. 47

1. my	7. their
2. her	8. your
3. my	9. his
4. Our	10. its
5. your	11. our
6. His	

Practice 2 p. 48

1. my	6. our
2. her	7. your
3. their	8. their
4. his	9. your
5. its	10. our

Nouns

PLURAL COUNT NOUNS

Practice 1 p. 49

matches

potatoes
eggs
paper towels

Practice 2 p. 50

1. sisters	7. costumes
2. glasses	8. Americans
3. chairs	9. teeth
4. children	10. boxes
5. fish	11. names
6. feet	

NONCOUNT NOUNS

Practice 1 pp. 51–52

1. an	7. X
2. X	8. an
3. any	9. X
4. a	10. some
5. X	11. X
6. any	

Practice 2 p. 52

1. salt
2. information
3. bread
4. help
5. alcohol
6. money
7. music
8. milk
9. fast food
10. traffic
11. rice

Future

FUTURE WITH *BE GOING TO*

Practice 1 p. 54
Example:
We <u>are going to have</u> visitors next week.
A: Next week my cousin and her family <u>are going to</u> come to Los Angeles.

B: What <u>are they going to do</u> here?
A: They<u>'re going to go</u> to Hollywood on Monday.
B: <u>Are you going to go</u> with them?
A: No, I <u>am going to stay</u> home that day. But on Tuesday, we<u>'re going to go</u> to the beach together.
B: What about your wife? <u>Is she going to</u> join you?
A: Yes, <u>she's going to</u> take the day off from work.
B: It sounds like <u>it's going to be</u> fun.
A: Definitely. And we can eat in restaurants. <u>I'm not going to cook</u>!

Practice 2 p. 54
Example:
It *'s going to rain / is going to rain*
A: 's going to have / is going to have
B: 's going to attend / is going to attend
A: isn't going to attend / is not going to attend
B: are you going to stay
A: 'm going to stay / am going to stay
B: Are your parents going to stay
A: 're going to stay / are going to stay
B: is going to be
A: 're going to eat / are going to eat
  'm not going to worry / am not going to worry

FUTURE WITH *WILL*

Practice 1 p. 56
Example:
1. We <u>will have</u> visitors next week.
2. Lunch <u>will be</u> ready in five minutes.
3. <u>Will it be</u> cold tonight?
4. Dr. Patterson <u>will not be</u> here tomorrow.
5. I think Serena Williams <u>will win</u> the tennis game.
6. The party <u>will start</u> at about 8:30.
7. If the weather is nice, <u>I will ride</u> my bike to work.

8. The next train <u>will come</u> in six minutes.

9. When <u>will Helena have</u> her baby?

10. I called the refrigerator repairman. <u>He'll be</u> here in an hour.

11. I promise <u>I won't be</u> late.

Practice 2 pp. 56–57

Example:

1. *It will be cold tonight.*

2. Al won't come to our party.

3. She will be out of town next week.

4. Will your brother be a doctor?

5. The price of gas will go up.

6. Our taxes will not come down.

7. When will he start his new job?

8. Who will help me?

9. I won't have an accident.

10. You will enjoy your trip to Cancún.

11. We will see you there.

FUTURE TIME EXPRESSIONS

Practice 1 pp. 57–58

1. b	7. b
2. a	8. a
3. b	9. a
4. b	10. a
5. a	11. a
6. b	

Practice 2 p. 59

1. this	7. this
2. next	8. in
3. this	9. next
4. in	10. in
5. In	11. this
6. Next	

Imperatives

Practice 1 p. 60

To cook perfect spaghetti or other pasta, [follow] these steps. First, [fill] a large pot with cold water and [let] it boil. [Don't cover] the pot with a lid.

When the water boils, [add] one or two tablespoons of salt. The salt will make the pasta taste better. [Don't add] oil.

[Cook] the pasta for 8–12 minutes. [Don't overcook] it. When it's ready, it will be soft but a little chewy. (The Italians call this "al dente.")

Next, [remove] the pot from the heat and [add] a cup of cold water. This will stop the cooking.

Now [drain] the pasta in the sink. Then [transfer] it to a bowl. Finally, [add] your favorite sauce.

Practice 2 p. 61

1. <u>Move</u> to a safe place.

2. If possible, <u>get</u> under a desk or table.

3. <u>Stay</u> away from windows and bookcases.

4. <u>Don't use</u> elevators.

5. <u>Don't go</u> outside until the shaking stops.

6. If you are in bed, <u>put</u> a pillow over your head to protect it.

7. If you are outdoors, <u>don't stand</u> near buildings or trees.

8. If you are driving, <u>pull</u> over to the side of the road.

Prepositions

PREPOSITIONS OF TIME

Practice 1 p. 63

1. at	6. In
2. On	7. in
3. at	8. on
4. from, to	9. for
5. on	10. in

Practice 2 p. 63

America's space shuttle program operated [for] 30 years, [from] 1981 [to] 2011. The shuttles flew into space and back. They carried astronauts and equipment.

The first space shuttle, *Columbia*, went into space [on] April 12, 1981. It completed 28 trips. It was in space [for] a total of 300 days. The last shuttle, *Atlantis*, completed its last flight [on] July 8, 2011.

Some of the "retired" shuttles are going to be in museums. For example, *Atlantis* will be at the Kennedy Space Center in Florida. The exhibit opened to the public [in] July 2013.

The shuttle *Endeavor* flew 25 missions [from] 1981 [to] 2011. Now visitors can see it at the California Science Center in Los Angeles. The exhibit opened [on] Tuesday, October 30, 2012.

PREPOSITIONS OF PLACE

Practice 1 pp. 64–65

1. a, 2. c, 3. c, 4. b, 5. b, 6. b, 7. a, 8. c, 9. b, 10. c

Practice 2 p. 66

1. on top of
2. in
3. across from
4. near
5. above
6. in the middle of
7. between
8. next to

Present

SIMPLE PRESENT *BE*

Practice 1 p. 68

1. is
2. are / 're
3. is / 's
4. are
5. is / 's
6. am / 'm
7. are
8. is / 's
9. is / 's
10. are / 're

Practice 2 p. 68

1. is / isn't
2. is not / 's not / isn't
3. are not / 're not / aren't
4. are not / 're not / aren't
5. are not / aren't
6. is not / 's not / isn't
7. are not / aren't
8. am not / 'm not
9. are not / aren't
10. are not / aren't

THE SIMPLE PRESENT

Practice 1 p. 70

1. like
2. have
3. believe
4. calls
5. has
6. sleep
7. speaks
8. study
9. washes
10. tastes
11. need

Practice 2 p. 70

1. doesn't walk / does not walk
2. doesn't like / does not like
3. don't feel / do not feel
4. doesn't snow / does not snow
5. doesn't have / does not have
6. doesn't understand / does not understand
7. don't want / do not want
8. doesn't sell / does not sell
9. don't speak / do not speak
10. don't need / do not need
11. don't know / do not know

FREQUENCY ADVERBS

Practice 1 p. 72

1. Never she is late.
2. Cathy eats dessert never.
3. Rarely the train is late.
4. Raul takes sometimes the bus to work.
5. Kei doesn't have usually an 8:00 A.M. class.
6. Mr. Holt eats breakfast at home rarely.
7. Ray sends text messages often during class.
8. Bus drivers in my town never are rude.
9. Often it doesn't rain in March.
10. Often Bella makes spelling mistakes.
11. Gina never is late to work.

Practice 2 p. 73

1. Georgia is never late to work.
2. My family always eats dinner together.
3. Linda usually finishes work at 5:30. / Usually Linda finishes work at 5:30.
4. My friends and I don't often study together.
5. Sometimes Marwan does not understand his teacher.
6. The mail is seldom late.
7. The restaurant is never open on Christmas.
8. My kids usually have activities after school. / Usually my kids have activities after school.
9. Mr. and Mrs. Short often go out for breakfast.
10. Susan's dog never barks.
11. Exercise is not always healthy.

PRESENT PROGRESSIVE

Practice 1 p. 75

1. is raining
2. are playing
3. is winning
4. are watching
5. is talking
6. I'm studying / am studying
7. is bothering
8. is having / 's having
9. Are you going
10. Is your sister coming
11. are you leaving

Practice 2 pp. 75–76

1. is not shining / isn't shining
2. is not raining / 's not raining / isn't raining
3. is not blowing / isn't blowing
4. are not wearing / aren't wearing
5. is not working / 's not working / isn't working

6. am not making / 'm not making
7. are not listening / 're not listening / aren't listening
8. are not jogging / 're not jogging / aren't jogging
9. are not smiling / 're not smiling / aren't smiling
10. are not running / aren't running
11. are not growing / aren't growing

SIMPLE PRESENT VS. PRESENT PROGRESSIVE

Practice 1 pp. 77–78

1. Incorrect	7. Correct
2. Incorrect	8. Incorrect
3. Correct	9. Incorrect
4. Incorrect	10. Correct
5. Incorrect	11. Incorrect
6. Incorrect	

Practice 2 pp. 78–79

1. don't need	7. is walking
2. is sleeping	8. don't have
3. has	9. is visiting
4. don't hear	10. don't see
5. am calling	11. grows
6. look	

Pronouns

SUBJECT PRONOUNS

Practice 1 pp. 80–81

1. b	5. a	9. a
2. a	6. a	10. a
3. a	7. b	
4. b	8. b	

Practice 2 p. 81

1. She	5. You	9. It
2. He	6. We	10. We
3. I	7. She	11. I
4. It	8. They	

OBJECT PRONOUNS

Practice 1 pp. 82–83

1. a, 2. b, 3. a, 4. b, 5. b, 6. a, 7. a, 8. b, 9. b, 10. a

Practice 2 p. 83

1. me	5. me	9. us
2. me	6. him	10. me
3. it	7. it	11. us
4. them	8. her	

Past

VERB *BE*

Practice 1 pp. 84–85

1. was	7. Was
2. were	8. was not
3. was	9. were
4. weren't	10. was not
5. was	11. Were
6. were	

Practice 2 p. 85

1. Where were you?
2. Yesterday, Gabriel was absent.
3. This morning, I was not late.
4. Were you confused?
5. When were you in your office?
6. Manya and I were ready for the test.
7. Sima was not in our group.
8. Was your interview on Thursday?
9. What was the correct answer?
10. Yesterday evening we were not home.
11. Who was the captain of the team?

REGULAR VERBS

Practice 1 pp. 86–87

1. waited	7. fixed
2. asked	8. hurried
3. decided	9. arrived
4. studied	10. preferred
5. stopped	11. visited
6. stayed	

Practice 2 p. 87

1. did not walk	8. did not wait
2. did not cook	9. did not watch
3. did not play	10. did not walk
4. did not rain	11. did not wash
5. did not talk	12. did not come
6. did not snow	13. did not write
7. did not go	

IRREGULAR VERBS

Practice 1 p. 89

Last night I studied until 10. Then I walked my dog.

I usually speak to my grandmother once a day. Yesterday evening I called her and we talked for about ten minutes. I told her I planned to come visit her in the morning. Then we said good night.

This morning I called my grandmother at about 9 a.m. To my surprise, she did not answer the phone. I waited half an hour, and then I tried again. Again there was no answer. I began to worry. What if she had an accident? I decided to go see her.

I got in my car and drove to her apartment. When I arrived, I knocked on her door and called her name. I was nervous. But 30 seconds later she opened the door.

"Grandma, are you OK?" I asked her.

"Yes, why?" she answered.

"Well, I called you three times this morning, and you didn't answer. What happened?"

"Nothing happened, dear. I stayed up half the night reading a book, so this morning I slept late. I just woke up. Would you like to come in and eat breakfast with me?"

Practice 2 p. 89

1. sold	7. saw
2. became	8. spent
3. broke	9. took
4. felt	10. taught
5. left	11. thought
6. made	

TIME EXPRESSIONS

Practice 1 pp. 90–91

1. Incorrect	7. Incorrect
2. Incorrect	8. Correct
3. Incorrect	9. Correct
4. Correct	10. Incorrect
5. Incorrect	11. Correct
6. Incorrect	

Practice 2 pp. 91–92

1. three years ago	7. for
2. Last	8. in
3. for	9. On
4. two years ago	10. ago
5. in	11. last week
6. on	

There is and *There are*

THERE IS / THERE ARE

Practice 1 p. 94

1. There are	7. There is
2. There is	8. There is
3. There are	9. There are
4. There are	10. There is
5. There is	11. There are
6. There is	

Practice 2 p. 94

1. There are	They are
They are	Their
2. There are	4. There are
Their	They are
They are	5. There are
3. There are	Their

SUBJECT-VERB AGREEMENTS WITH *THERE IS / THERE ARE*

Practice 1 pp. 95–96

1. are	4. is	7. is
2. is	5. are	8. is
3. are	6. is	9. are

Practice 2 pp. 96–97

1. There is	7. There are no
2. There is	8. There is no
3. There are	9. There is
4. There are	10. There is
5. There is no	11. There are no
6. There is	

SENTENCE STRUCTURE

Coordinating Conjunctions

COORDINATING CONJUNCTION AND

Practice 1 pp. 98–99

1. Jenna and Larry are from Boston.
2. Oranges and strawberries have / Strawberries and oranges have
3. runs and lifts weights / lifts weights and runs
4. bought a bag of potatoes and a loaf of
5. is cold and sweet / is sweet and cold / 's cold and sweet / 's sweet and cold
6. Chile and Peru are in / Peru and Chile are in
7. talks quickly and loudly / talks loudly and quickly
8. Horses and cows can swim / Cows and horses can swim
9. likes pop music and jazz / likes jazz and pop music
10. Marta and her mother sell toys
11. in Minnesota are cold and wet / in Minnesota are wet and cold

Practice 2 pp. 99–100

1. a big dog, and his name is
2. was tired, and she began
3. is cooking dinner, and Jane is watching
4. in the daytime, and he goes to school

5. on Monday, and it snowed
6. walks to school, and Don rides
7. has an iPod, and he takes it
8. was a fire, and many houses
9. a flute, and I'm learning how
10. forgot to water the plant, and it
11. late, and it's time to

COORDINATING CONJUNCTION *BUT*

Practice 1 pp. 100–101

1. Sandy is small but strong.
2. She talks quickly but clearly.
3. The day was cold but clear.
4. My dogs are big but gentle.
5. The test was long but easy.
6. The food was simple but tasty.
7. Our teacher is strict but fair.
8. Thomas is smart but disorganized.
9. Mark drives quickly but carefully.
10. The course was difficult but useful.
11. Roller coasters are scary but exciting.

Practice 2 pp. 101–102

1. Charles [likes cats, but he doesn't like] dogs.
2. I want [to go with you, but I have] to study.
3. David works [in the city, but he doesn't live] there.
4. The furniture [is expensive, but it is not / is expensive, but it's not] comfortable.
5. The flowers [are pretty, but they smell] bad.
6. The music [was great, but it was too] loud.
7. [The work is hard, but it is / The work is hard, but it's] interesting.
8. Sharon [loves to eat, but she hates to] cook.
9. The shoes [were ugly, but they were] comfortable.
10. I sent [Tomiko a message, but she didn't] reply.
11. Peter only [slept three hours, but he isn't] tired.

COORDINATING CONJUNCTION *OR*

Practice 1 p. 103

1. Joyce likes [Italian or Thousand Island / Thousand Island or Italian] dressing.
2. [Zach or Rina / Rina or Zach] will bring a cake.
3. Steven [swims or runs 3 miles / runs 3 miles or swims] every day.
4. We're going to have [pizza or hamburgers / hamburgers or pizza].
5. Katrina will buy a [sports car or a motorcycle / a motorcycle or a sports car].
6. [Dr. Haas or Dr. Cheng / Dr. Cheng or Dr. Haas] can help you.
7. She eats [scrambled eggs or cereal / cereal or scrambled eggs] every morning.
8. I like spaghetti with [tomato or pesto / pesto or tomato] sauce.
9. Susan [reads the newspaper or listens to the news / listens to the news or reads the newspaper] before work.
10. Marta or her mother will walk the dog.
11. Linda will [phone or email / email or phone] her mother.

Practice 2 pp. 103–104

1. I will go home by bus, or I will walk.
2. Are you from Italy, or are you from France?
3. Jane will stay in school, or [she will / she'll] get a job.
4. Mehdi will do the project alone, or [he will / he'll] find a partner
5. I'll wear an old dress, or I'll buy something new.

6. We can carpool, or we can meet at the restaurant.

7. They will look for a cheap hotel, or [they will / they'll] camp out.

8. Maria is telling the truth, or [she is / she's] lying.

9. I can make a salad, or I can set the table.

10. The war will end, or more people will die.

11. We can work until 6, or we can go home now.

COORDINATING CONJUNCTION SO

Practice 1 p. 105

1. Incorrect
2. Correct
3. Incorrect
4. Correct
5. Incorrect
6. Correct
7. Correct
8. Incorrect
9. Incorrect
10. Incorrect

Practice 2 p. 105

Part 1

1. I don't want to eat.
2. He can't do his homework.
3. He always sits near the teacher.
4. She is very tired.
5. We got lost.

Part 2

1. I'm not hungry, so I don't want to eat.
2. Mike lost his textbook, so he can't do his homework.
3. Jeff cannot hear well, so he always sits near the teacher.
4. Sheila has a new baby, so she is very tired.
5. We got wrong directions to the theater, so we got lost.

Subordinating Conjunctions

SUBORDINATING CONJUNCTION IF

Practice 1 p. 106

1. Incorrect
2. Incorrect
3. Correct
4. Incorrect
5. Incorrect
6. Incorrect
7. Incorrect
8. Correct

Practice 2 p. 107

1. If I have time, I will go jogging.
2. If I study hard, I will get good grades.
3. I will get a part-time job if I need money.
4. If Joe gets a job, he will buy a car.
5. I will miss you if you move away.
6. If I get an A on my test, my parents will be proud.
7. If you do not answer your phone, I will leave a message. / If you don't answer your phone, I will leave a message.
8. I will walk to work if the weather is nice.
9. If we are late, the boss will be angry.

SUBORDINATING CONJUNCTION BECAUSE

Practice 1 p. 108

1. Correct
2. Incorrect
3. Correct
4. Incorrect
5. Correct
6. Incorrect
7. Correct
8. Incorrect

Practice 2 pp. 108–109

1. a We didn't have class because the teacher was absent.

   b Because the teacher was absent, we didn't have class.

2. a Because I'm not hungry, I don't want to eat.

   b I don't want to eat because I'm not hungry.

3. a Bob and Sheila are always tired because they have a new baby.

b Because Bob and Sheila have a new baby, they're always tired.

4. a We were late because traffic was very bad.

   b Because traffic was very bad, we were late.

5. a My car didn't start because the battery was dead.

   b Because the battery was dead, my car didn't start.

6. a I got 90% on my test because you helped me study.

   b Because you helped me study, I got 90% on my test.

7. a I opened the window because the room was hot.

   b Because the room was hot, I opened the window.

8. a Henry did not laugh because the joke was not funny.

   b Because the joke was not funny, Henry did not laugh.

9. a Barbara eats a lot of fast food because she doesn't enjoy cooking.

   b Because she doesn't enjoy cooking, Barbara eats a lot of fast food.

SUBORDINATING CONJUNCTION *BEFORE*, *AFTER*, AND *WHEN*

Practice 1 pp. 110–111

1. after he is 65
2. I will eat dinner
3. after she graduates from college
4. after you leave
5. the dog barked
6. she called her husband
7. After he went swimming
8. Right after I eat too much
9. it got very cold
10. after the plane landed
11. Peter was very lonely

Practice 2 pp. 111–112

1. When I'm tired, I go to bed early. OR I go to bed early when I'm tired.

2. After I finish dinner, I will wash the dishes. OR I will wash the dishes after I finish dinner. OR I'll wash the dishes after I finish dinner. OR After I finish dinner, I'll wash the dishes.

3. We will eat when the chicken is ready. OR When the chicken is ready, we will eat. OR We'll eat when the chicken is ready. OR When the chicken is ready, we'll eat.

4. Before we go to bed, we turn off the lights. OR We turn off the lights before we go to bed.

5. Before I went to school, I didn't know how to read. OR I didn't know how to read before I went to school.

6. When the concert ended, the musicians left the stage. OR The musicians left the stage when the concert ended.

7. Before I go to work, I eat breakfast. OR I eat breakfast before I go to work.

8. After Chantal graduated from college, she went to law school. OR Chantal went to law school after she graduated from college.

9. When I stay up late, I get tired. OR I get tired when I stay up late.

10. Check your test paper before you turn it in. OR Before you turn it in, check your test paper.

11. After Jane sold her house, she moved to Florida. OR Jane moved to Florida after she sold her house.

The Sentence

SUBJECT AND VERB

Practice 1 pp. 113–114

1. c, 2. a, 3. c, 4. c, 5. b, 6. a, 7. c, 8. c, 9. b

Practice 2 pp. 114–115

1. No verb
2. Correct
3. No verb
4. No subject
5. Correct
6. No verb
7. No subject
8. No subject
9. Correct

SUBJECT, VERB, OBJECT

Practice 1 p. 115

1. a novel
2. piano
3. tired
4. tomatoes
5. a famous cello player
6. Spanish
7. the window
8. a cake
9. gymnasts
10. economics
11. a British colony

Practice 2 pp. 116–117

1. I lost my phone.
2. Chandra speaks three languages.
3. A mechanic fixed my car.
4. Wynton Marsalis plays the trumpet.
5. Katya's boyfriend is very quiet.
6. Joyce's job is boring.
7. Professor Baker corrected our compositions.
8. Jackie doesn't have a smart phone.
9. A pediatrician is a doctor for children.
10. Serdar married his sister's friend.

RUN-ON SENTENCES

Practice 1 p. 118

1. Run-on
2. Run-on
3. Run-on
4. OK
5. Run-on
6. Run-on
7. Run-on
8. Run-on
9. OK

Practice 2 p. 118

1. I had a bad morning, everything went wrong.
   I cut myself shaving, I burned my breakfast.
   I hope tomorrow will be better it can't be worse!

2. I'm going to graduate from New York University in 2015 then I will return to my country.
   I want to get an MBA degree after I can manage my father's company.
   I will manage the company my father will retire.

SUBJECT-VERB AGREEMENT

Practice 1 pp. 119–120

1. are
2. smells
3. is
4. are
5. are
6. is
7. drives
8. drive
9. is
10. sounds
11. are

Practice 2 p. 120

1. are
2. hurts
3. know
4. is
5. gives
6. need
7. have
8. have
9. is
10. comes
11. is

Parts of Speech

COMMON AND PROPER NOUNS

Practice 1 p. 121

place, vacation, sister, family, island, beach, sun, day, home, winter, friends, tan

Practice 2 p. 122

1. Anna
2. Chicago
3. Picasso
4. Cubism
5. Paris
6. France
7. Louvre
8. Madrid
9. Picasso's
10. Guernica

VERBS

Practice 1 p. 122

1. live
2. is
3. has
4. are

5. like   8. have
6. eat   9. babysit
7. watch   10. help

Practice 2 p. 123

1. Incorrect   6. Incorrect
2. Incorrect   7. Correct
3. Correct   8. Incorrect
4. Incorrect   9. Correct
5. Correct

ADJECTIVES

Practice 1 p. 124

small, coffee, tired, bored, nice, comfortable, delicious, wonderful, friendly, interesting

Practice 2 p. 125

1. b, 2. a, 3. b, 4. b, 5. b, 6. b, 7. a, 8. a, 9. a, 10. b

PARAGRAPH ORGANIZATION

Topic Sentence

Practice 1 p. 126

1. they are generous and hardworking
2. are fashionable and comfortable
3. is important for strong bones and teeth
4. "Arabica" and "robusta."
5. Because they eat insects
6. have long arms and big feet
7. are not "true" nuts
8. is Cozumel, Mexico
9. It's easy and fun
10. are very bad for your feet and legs
11. two important facts

Practice 2 p. 127

1. b   2. b   3. a

Ordering

TIME ORDER

Practice 1 p. 129

Paragraph 1: To begin; Second; Third; Next; Finally

Paragraph 2: To begin, Then, Third, Last

Practice 2 pp. 129–130

Paragraph 1

2 Second, take a deep breath and hold it.

5 After you take the first sip, drink some more small sips for 20 or 30 seconds. Be sure to hold your breath the whole time.

6 Finally, stand up and breathe out. Your hiccups will be gone.

1 First, fill a tall glass with water.

4 Next, take a small sip of water from the far side of the glass. If you sip from the far side, the water will not spill.

3 Third, bend over and hold the glass of water under your mouth.

Paragraph 2

3 After he reads, he works in his garden for one or two hours.

2 Next, he has breakfast and reads the newspaper.

5 Later in the day, he goes shopping, visits his parents, or goes to the movie with a friend.

6 Finally, he comes home and gets ready for work the next day.

4 Then he goes back inside and eats lunch.

1 First, he takes a shower and shaves.

LISTING ORDER

Practice 1 p. 131

There are three reasons why I want to be a nurse.

Follow these few suggestions to save money on your monthly water bill.

Riding my bicycle to work has several advantages.

There are three easy things you can do to lower your blood pressure.

There are three reasons why I do not have a smart phone.

A good teacher needs to have four important qualities.

Practice 2 pp. 131–132

Paragraph 1: First of all,; Second,; In addition,; Finally,

Paragraph 2: First,; Also,; Most important

Paragraph 3: For one thing,; Also,; Third,; Last,

SPACE ORDER

Practice 1 pp. 132–133

1. west to east
2. front to back
3. inside to outside

Practice 2 pp. 133–134

1. From north to south, the Pacific states are Washington, Oregon, and California.
2. In Tanzania, a common style of house is the Swahili house.
3. There are a number of interesting old buildings on Pine Avenue, my town's main street.

Supporting Sentences

PROVIDING REASONS

Practice 1 pp. 135–136

Paragraph 1: First of all; Second; Also; Finally

Paragraph 2: One reason is; Another reason is; The third reason is

Paragraph 3: First of all; Second; Another reason; Last

Practice 2 pp. 136–137

Paragraph 1

3 Also, I don't need a smart phone. I work at home, and I don't go out very much. I can use my computer to get information or check my email.

2 First of all, smart phones are expensive. The phone is more than $200, and the monthly service plan is very expensive. I can't afford it.

4 Finally, I don't have a smart phone because I am lazy. I don't enjoy learning about new technology. I have a cell phone, a laptop computer, a camera, an iPod, and an ebook reader. That's enough technology for me!

1 There are three reasons why I don't own a smart phone.

5 I hope now you understand why I don't want and don't need a smart phone.

Paragraph 2

4 The third reason I love swimming is that the water feels good. It is cool and clean. It makes my skin feel smooth.

2 The first reason is that swimming is a gentle sport. There is no running or jumping, so I cannot hurt myself when I swim.

1 I love swimming for four reasons.

5 Finally, I love swimming because it is a quiet sport. There is almost no noise in the pool. It's my favorite place to think.

3 Second, swimming is good for my muscles. It is especially good for stretching my back and shoulders. Because I swim, I never have pain in my back.

6 All these reasons explain why swimming is my favorite sport.

USING DETAILS

Practice 1 p. 138

1. Louis Braille is buried in Paris.
2. She has a dirty old Toyota.
3. Some people are allergic to cats.

Practice 2 pp. 138–139

1. a, b, d
2. a, c, e
3. a, b, d

GIVING EXAMPLES

Practice 1 p. 140

1. a   2. c   3. b   4. a   5. c

Practice 2 pp. 140–141

1. For example, she loves tomatoes.
2. For example (*or* For instance), she eats leftover
3. For example (*or* For instance), it tells me the weather
4. For example (*or* For instance), he volunteers at a children's
5. For example (*or* For instance), Chinese verbs
6. For example (*or* For instance), two lily leaves
7. For example (*or* For instance), every Sunday she makes
8. For example (*or* For instance), he often locks
9. For example (*or* For instance), he never forgets
10. For example (*or* For instance), you can use it
11. For example (*or* For instance), she speaks

The Conclusion

Practice 1 p. 142

1. c   2. b   3. b

Practice 2 p. 143

1. a   2. c   3. a

Unity

Practice 1 pp. 144–145

1. c   2. b   3. a

Practice 2 p. 145

1. Summer is the busy tourist season in London.
2. Columbus introduced corn to Europe.
3. One time he forgot his cello in a taxi.

Writing Assignments p. 146—165

Answers will vary.

POST-TEST

Post-Test 1 pp. 177–182

1. b, 2. c, 3. d, 4. d, 5. b, 6. c, 7. c, 8. d,
9. c, 10. c, 11. b, 12. a, 13. b, 14. c,
15. b, 16. c, 17. d, 18. d, 19. d, 20. c,
21. c, 22. d, 23. a, 24. c, 25. a, 26. c,
27. b, 28. a, 29. d, 30. d, 31. a, 32. a,
33. d, 34. b, 35. b, 36. a, 37. d, 38. c,
39. d, 40. b

Post-Test 2 p. 183

Answers will vary.